The Little
of Explorations

by Sally Featherstone
Illustrations by Mike Phillips

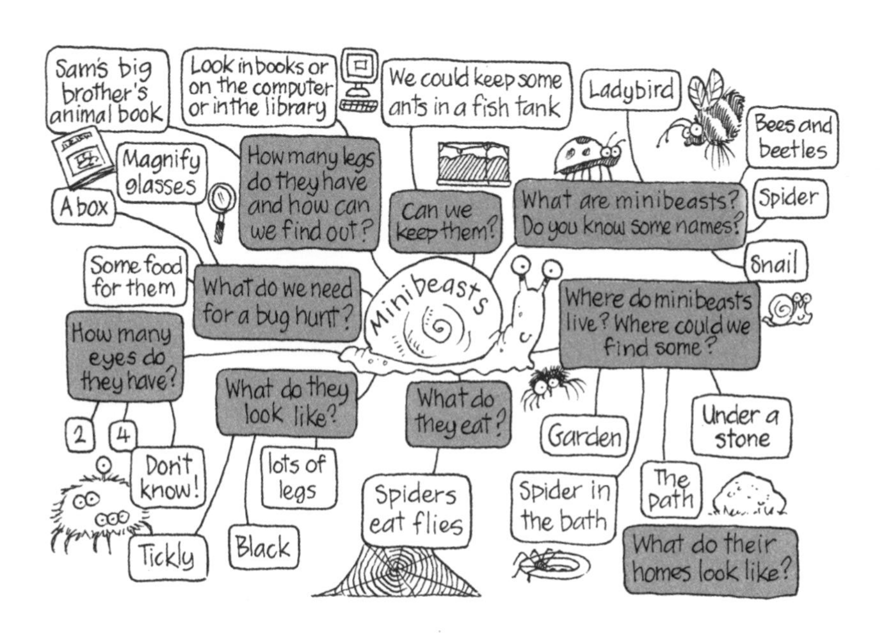

LITTLE BOOKS WITH **BIG** IDEAS

This edition published 2013 by Featherstone, an imprint of Bloomsbury Publishing Plc
Published 2010 by A&C Black, an imprint of Bloomsbury Publishing Plc
50 Bedford Square, London WC1B 3DP
www.bloomsbury.com

ISBN 978-1-4729-0252-8

A CIP record for this publication is available from the British Library.

Printed in Great Britain by Latimer Trend & Company Limited

This book is produced using paper that is made from wood grown in managed, sustainable forests. It is natural, renewable and recyclable.

The logging and manufacturing processes conform to the environmental regulations of the country of origin.

10 9 8 7 6 5 4 3 2 1

Contents

Introduction

This book is one of the titles in a series of Little Books, which explore aspects of practice within the Early Years Foundation Stage in England. The books are also suitable for practitioners working with the early years curriculum in Wales, Northern Ireland and Scotland, and in any early years setting catering for young children.

Across the series you will find titles appropriate to each aspect of the curriculum for children from two to five years, giving practitioners a wealth of ideas for engaging activities, interesting resources and stimulating environments to enrich their work across the Early Years Curriculum.

Each title also has information linking the activity pages to the statutory Early Years curriculum for England. This title has been updated to include the revised Early Learning Goals published by the Department for Education in March 2012. The full set of 19 goals is included in the introduction to each book, and the activity pages will refer you to the relevant statements to which each activity contributes.

For the purposes of observation and assessment of the children's work in each activity, we recommend that practitioners should use each of the 'revised statements' as a whole, resisting any impulse to separate the elements of each one into short phrases.

The key goals for this title are highlighted in purple, although other goals may be included on some pages.

PRIME AREAS

Communication and language

① **Listening and attention:** children listen attentively in a range of situations. They listen to stories, accurately anticipating key events and respond to what they hear with relevant comments, questions or actions. They give their attention to what others say and respond appropriately, while engaged in another activity.

② **Understanding:** children follow instructions involving several ideas or actions. They answer 'how' and 'why' questions about their experiences and in response to stories or events.

③ **Speaking:** children express themselves effectively, showing awareness of listeners' needs. They use past, present and future forms accurately when talking about events that have happened or are to happen in the future. They develop their own narratives and explanations by connecting ideas or events.

Physical development

① **Moving and handling:** children show good control and co-ordination in large and small movements. They move confidently in a range of ways, safely negotiating space. They handle equipment and tools effectively, including pencils for writing.

② **Health and self-care:** children know the importance for good health of physical exercise, and a healthy diet, and talk about ways to keep healthy and safe. They manage their own basic hygiene and personal needs successfully, including dressing and going to the toilet independently.

Personal, social and emotional development

① **Self-confidence and self-awareness:** children are confident to try new activities, and say why they like some activities more than others. They are confident to speak in a familiar group, will talk about their ideas, and will choose the resources they need for their chosen activities. They say when they do or don't need help.

② **Managing feelings and behaviour:** children talk about how they and others show feelings, talk about their own and others' behaviour, and its consequences, and know that some behaviour is unacceptable. They work as part of a group or class, and understand and follow the rules. They adjust their behaviour to different situations, and take changes of routine in their stride.

③ **Making relationships:** children play co-operatively, taking turns with others. They take account of one another's ideas about how to organise their activity. They show sensitivity to others' needs and feelings, and form positive relationships with adults and other children.

SPECIFIC AREAS

Literacy

① **Reading:** children read and understand simple sentences. They use phonic knowledge to decode regular words and read them aloud accurately. They also read some common irregular words. They demonstrate understanding when talking with others about what they have read.

② **Writing:** children use their phonic knowledge to write words in ways which match their spoken sounds. They also write some irregular common words. They write simple sentences which can be read by themselves and others. Some words are spelt correctly and others are phonetically plausible.

Mathematics

① **Numbers:** children count reliably with numbers from 1 to 20, place them in order and say which number is one more or one less than a given number. Using quantities and objects, they add and subtract two single-digit numbers and count on or back to find the answer. They solve problems, including doubling, halving and sharing.

② **Shape, space and measures:** children use everyday language to talk about size, weight, capacity, position, distance, time and money to compare quantities and objects and to solve problems. They recognise, create and describe patterns. They explore characteristics of everyday objects and shapes and use mathematical language to describe them.

Understanding the world

① **People and communities:** children talk about past and present events in their own lives and in the lives of family members. They know that other children don't always enjoy the same things, and are sensitive to this. They know about similarities and differences between themselves and others, and among families, communities and traditions.

② **The world:** children know about similarities and differences in relation to places, objects, materials and living things. They talk about the features of their own immediate environment and how environments might vary from one another. They make observations of animals and plants and explain why some things occur, and talk about changes.

③ **Technology:** children recognise that a range of technology is used in places such as homes and schools. They select and use technology for particular purposes.

Expressive arts and design

① **Exploring and using media and materials:** children sing songs, make music and dance, and experiment with ways of changing them. They safely use and explore a variety of materials, tools and techniques, experimenting with colour, design, texture, form and function.

② **Being imaginative:** children use what they have learnt about media and materials in original ways, thinking about uses and purposes. They represent their own ideas, thoughts and feelings through design and technology, art, music, dance, role-play and stories.

This exploration contributes to the following Goals for the EYFS:

PRIME

Communication and Language ① ③
Physical Development ① ②
PSED ① ② ③

SPECIFIC

Mathematics ① ②
Understanding of the World ① ② ③
Expressive arts and design ① ②

This book is one of the titles in a series of Little Books, which explore aspects of practice within the Early Years Foundation Stage in England. The books are also suitable for practitioners working with the early years curriculum in Wales, Northern Ireland and Scotland, and in any early years setting catering for young children.

Across the series you will find titles appropriate to each aspect of the curriculum for children from two to five years, giving practitioners a wealth of ideas for engaging activities, interesting resources and stimulating environments to enrich their work across the Early Years Curriculum.

Each title also has information linking the activity pages to the statutory Early Years curriculum for England. This title has been updated to include the revised Early Learning Goals published by the Department for Education in March 2012. The full set of 19 goals is included in the introduction to each book, and the activity pages will refer you to the relevant statements to which each activity contributes.

For the purposes of observation and assessment of the children's work in each activity, we recommend that practitioners should use each of the Revised Statements as a whole, resisting any impulse to separate the elements of each one into short phrases.

The key goals for this book are presented in heavy type below.

The Little Book of Investigations has been one of the most popular titles in the Little Books series. The Little Book of Explorations will help you to extend investigations over a longer period, from a few weeks to a whole year. Of course you won't be following the same exploration all the time during this longer period, but children will learn much more about a topic if they return to it after a period of time, to top up knowledge, to look at different aspects, to meet different people, or to see places at different times of the year. A 'bug hunt' in the summer will reveal very different creatures from a 'bug hunt' in the winter; a park visit in the winter will involve children in expanding the activities they were involved in during summer visits.

Each of the examples in this Little Book suggests that an 'ideas map' might help you and the children to establish what they already know about the exploration focus, and some of the things they might want to find out. The ideas map can be constructed during the talking time discussion, usually by an adult, to record what the children say and the things they already know. The map can also include resources, books and other places that the children suggest. As the discussion continues, further branches can be drawn and further information added, either in words, pictures, or a combination of both. Here is an example of what an ideas map might look like after a discussion of 'What is a minibeast?':

You will find some starter questions for your ideas map at the beginning of each exploration. Construct these maps during talking time, using felt pens on big pieces of paper, adding simple pictures to the words where you can, or offering the children the chance to add their own pictures. Make the map part of your display for each exploration. Keep the maps between the different parts of your exploration, and revisit them, talking them through and adding the new discoveries and new activities you want to plan.

When you have done your map, you could make a more detailed plan of all the possible pathways the exploration might take, and think how you could build them into a term or a year. Don't forget that the children's ideas and things that happen along the way may well make you change the order or the coverage, so don't set these plans in stone!

Use photo books, stories and other texts, visits and presentations, to keep the children's interest in the exploration alive as time goes on. Or take the opportunities offered by weather, animal life, or local events as the trigger to revive the exploration later in the term or the year. Have another talking time, look at your first ideas map and set off again!

The book is suitable for children from aged three in the Early Years Foundation Stage and can be extended into Key Stage 1. If you are working with younger children, you will need to take the explorations more slowly and simplify the activities appropriately.

Planning

The process described in this book proposes that you start each exploration with a 'talking time' – a discussion with the children of the exploration you are going to undertake. The ten examples in the book will give you some ideas, but of course there are hundreds of ways of starting an exploration, and thousands of things to explore. An exploration can be sparked by:

- a significant event for one of the children, such as a new baby in the family, moving house or going to hospital

- a celebration or community event such as a fair, a circus or a festival
- finding a snail, a ladybird or a beetle
- the weather or the seasons
- a question asked by a child, or by you.

Plan a celebration at a suitable point during or at the end of your exploration. This could be a party or picnic, a final visit to the woods or park, a display or presentation for parents or other children in your setting, or a selection of relevant photos and PowerPoint presentations for children to take home.

Prepare well

Before you start, and certainly before you plan to take the children on any walk or visit, plan carefully – make a visit yourself to check, not just for risks and potential problems, but for opportunities and starting points. Any visit will be a much richer experience if you are confident and knowledgeable about the area.

Some tips for your initial visit:

- Don't rush your preparation visit. Walk slowly, at the pace of a group of children, and include the walk from your setting or the bus or train stop. This will give you time to look around and see what the children might spot.
- Locate the toilets, find out about good spots for snack time or picnics, and any places where you could shelter from rain, wind or cold – some of your explorations will be in colder weather, maybe even in snow!
- Try to talk to the people who manage or work in the place you plan to visit. Approach the park wardens, woodland managers or rangers, shopkeepers and store managers, and local people who may let you look at their houses, gardens, or places of worship. These people will often be very keen to be involved if they know you are coming and have some ideas about what the children might discover. Some may be able to come with the children on your explorations and may become friends of your setting, offering other opportunities, resources and ideas.
- Try to get down to children's eye level to see what they will be able to see. This may give you ideas of things they may be interested in, and may also give you some surprises!
- Collect some of the resources you might need, particularly those that the children have suggested.

Involve the children and their families

All the explorations in this book have suggestions of ways to involve the children in the planning and organising of the ideas, visits, and follow-up activities.

The first way is to talk about the focus of the exploration, recording what the children suggest and what they already know in an ideas map. Use the suggested starter questions provided at the beginning of each section and add to these with some of your own. Give the children plenty of time to think, listen carefully to their suggestions and record these accurately.

Children love to be involved in preparations for activities and particularly for visits and excursions. These are great opportunities for drawing and writing lists together before collecting the things you need.

Listen to their suggestions for resources for the exploration – they may have different or even better ideas for resources and equipment to make the exploration enjoyable and fruitful. Of course you will want to add some resources that the children may not have used before, may not think of, or need practice in using. Your job is to expand and enhance the opportunities that each exploration offers.

Once your exploration is under way, the children will need to revisit stories, visits and other experiences in child-initiated or free flow play. Role-play is one way of doing this, and each of the explorations in this book suggests ways of making the exploration real by offering role-play resources and spaces, both in full body role-play, and in small world play. The adult-led visits and other stimuli can also be expanded in further adult-led or adult-initiated activities, some of which are included in each section. Towards the end of each of the explorations you will find extension ideas, and more questions to pose as you continue or return to each idea.

Don't worry if some children are more involved than others, there are always watchers and children whose interests may not follow the suggested path at that time. Revisiting the exploration later by having another talking time on the same focus will give these children further opportunities to be involved, perhaps at a time when they are more confident or receptive to the focus.

Don't forget to involve parents as helpers, experts, visitors and supporters of the explorations at home.

Stories and website resources

In each section there are a few ideas for finding images (such as photos, clipart) and a selection of useful websites.

At the end of each exploration you will find a booklist with a range of relevant fiction and non-fiction books for young children.

The explorations in this book will also contribute to the Characteristics of Effective Learning:

Playing and exploring

Active learning

Creating and thinking critically

Explore your setting

What can we find out about in our nursery/school? Focus: The local community

This is a good investigation to start a year with. It will give you and the children plenty of scope for real exploration, without having to leave your site. It's suitable for large or small settings and helps children to settle in when they are new.

Talking time

Talk about your nursery or school. Do the children know who works there? Do they know their way around? Do they know what is in all the rooms and cupboards? Well, now is the time to find out! Explain that you are going to explore your nursery or school and see how much you can find out by being detectives.

As you talk, make an ideas map together and note what the children already know and what they want to find out. Here are some starter ideas for discussion – you will be able to think of more!

The first exploration:

- **Ask the children if you need to take anything with you** on your exploration. Be prepared for a suggestion of magnifying glasses, and make sure you take a camera.
- **Talk about how to behave** when you are in someone else's room, and make sure the children know they can only do this sort of wandering and exploration with an adult, or when you give them permission.
- **Now take a walk together** around your setting or school. Go in more than one group if that works better or your school is very big, and share the information you gather. Make sure you warn your colleagues that you are coming so that they can be ready for the questions and explorations.
- **Make sure you go to as many places as you can.** If the school or setting you work in is big, you may want to split up, some doing the outside, some the inside, or some doing one part. Include these if they are part of the place where you work:
  - The staff room
  - The adult toilets (make sure they are empty!)
  - The kitchen if you have one
  - The caretaker or cleaner's room
  - The car park
  - The playgrounds for older children
  - The older children's classrooms or nurseries
  - The library
  - The store rooms for outdoor equipment or stationery
  - The storage areas for wheeled toys or PE equipment
  - The first aid or rest rooms
  - The dining hall or gym if you have one

- **Don't forget to take a camera** and ask people whether they mind having their photo taken. Take some photos of your children in these places too. This will help them to remember what happened and where they went.

Points to consider as you plan your exploration:

If you work in a large setting or school, or your setting is part of a larger organisation such as a leisure centre or community building, consider whether it is reasonable or useful to cover the whole building in one visit. Younger children will get much more from several small visits, and in this way you will be able to:

- Meet more people (some buildings support a large number of people).
- Look at parts of the building in action for different purposes (PE, dance, assembly and meals in a school hall, yoga, fitness, basketball, indoor football in a sports centre, groups for the elderly, parents and toddlers, painting classes in a community centre).
- Visit the spaces when they are empty. Children will be able to explore them much more easily and these spaces will seem very different.
- Look at the storage areas and other objects in the room. Encourage the children to respect the property of others, while taking time to look carefully at what they find.

While you are there:

Stay long enough for the children to really take in each area. BUT if they are getting tired or seem overwhelmed, cut the tour short and go back later to finish it. New people and places can be very stressful.

Don't forget to look at corridors and other spaces as you pass. Take in displays of children's work and other objects such as vases, plants, pieces of furniture and art works such as sculptures, paintings and glass objects. Look out of windows and doorways and open cupboards.

Spend time talking with the children about what they can see. Listen to their ideas about what they want to see, what they find, and what interests them. Let them choose where they want to go next and what they would like to look at. It is surprising what children notice and find fascinating, so give them some choice and time to explore.

Take as many cameras as you can collect (don't forget that most mobile phones now take photos) and make sure that you and the children take lots of photos of the things they are interested in. Take photos of the children as well as the places and things you see.

Remember to visit the less obvious parts of your setting, such as the kitchen, staff room or toilets. Don't forget meeting rooms, store cupboards and parts that are used by staff, parents and the community. Look at the places where staff make a cup of tea or have a rest.

Make a point of looking at cleaners' and premises officers' stores and cupboards (you may need to ask for a key and permission!) and point out that someone cleans and tidies the setting after the children have gone home.

Look for the letter box, the telephone, and the doorbell or other security devices. Photograph signs, words and labels around the building.

Go outside and look at all the places where the children don't usually go. Some will be used by other children or adults, some will be for services such as car parks and dustbin areas. Take photos of these as well, to remind the children of what they saw.

When you get back you could:

- Download and look at the photos you have taken. Talk about where the photos were taken, who the children met, what they saw, and what the different parts of the building are used for. If you have an interactive whiteboard, you could look at them together, and discuss them.
- If you have a computer, you could easily make the photos into a PowerPoint presentation, adding the children's words, so the children can watch it at any time.
- As you talk about your setting and the building it is in, ask some open questions about the building and grounds:
  - Where do the cars park?
  - Why do the cleaners come after we have gone home?
  - Where would you go if you felt poorly, who would look after you?
  - Who opens the letters that come here?
  - Who answers the phone if it rings?
  - Why are the rubbish bins near the kitchen door? Why can't we play near them?
  - Who buys all the paper and paint? Where is it kept?
  - Why is the hall so big?

Some adult-initiated activities:

- You could start to make a simple plan of your setting on a very big piece of paper, or a shower curtain, dust-sheet or piece of carpet. Draw pictures or stick photos of all the different places and things in the park, joining these by drawing paths and tracks between them so the children can follow the different routes around the building. Start with your room in the middle, then add the outdoor area you use, and work out from there, adding different parts of the building as you visit them.
- Make a photo book of all the adults and children who come to your setting. Have a page for each person, then add their name and role in the setting.
- Make flap books. They could be:
  - 'Who works in this room?' with a photo of the door on the flap and a photo of the person under the flap.
  - 'What's in this cupboard?' with a photo of the door and a photo of the things kept inside (cleaning resources, office equipment, staff cups and plates etc.) under the flap. You could even have a second flap for the person who uses the things in the cupboard.
  - Use your photos to make matching cards, the room and the person who works there, or Snap cards of the people's faces for quick recognition of who is who. Include the children's own faces.
  - Make recordings of sounds around your setting for a listening game.

Extensions into child-initiated learning (stimuli for children who are interested in replaying the experience):

- Leave the materials available for children to draw their own plans.
- Run off copies of photos of the adults and children for independent picture and book making.
- Offer Play people or Lego characters with bricks and other construction materials so children can replay their explorations of their own setting. You can buy bags of Play people or Lego children and play equipment to make settings or classrooms with outside spaces.

- Make a role-play area of part of your building. This could be a gym, health centre, library or an office. Ask the children what they need to make the space.
- Talk about how cleaners and premises officers work, and the equipment they use. Pretend to be them with old shirts as overalls and plenty of brooms and dustpans and dusters.

And together you could find out about other schools and nurseries by looking at or downloading some images from Google, or visiting some websites:

Google searches – day nursery, day nursery plan, health centre, fitness centre, community centre, Surestart centre, school office, cleaner, school, school plan, nursery, nursery garden. If you want to see who does what in a school or setting enter the name of the job (premises officer, secretary, receptionist, teacher, sports centre manager, nursery nurse etc.) in Google images and get some new faces!

Websites – http://www.forestschools.com - the home of the Forest School organisation

http://www.ltl.org.uk Learning Through Landscapes, a charity for improving educational provision out of doors.

Enter your local town name and 'schools', 'daycare' or 'nursery' in a search engine such as Google, and you should find a list and a map of the schools in your area.

Further experiences and visits to keep the interest alive:

- Go on an ICT walk round the setting, spotting all the things that communicate or give information e.g. microwave, photocopier, telephone, entry system, camera, security doors etc.
- Explore the colours, textures and patterns in your setting. Take some close-up photos of textures and surfaces as well as the whole object and play matching games or 'What is this?'
- Take photos of parts of familiar objects, such as a phone, a tap, a door handle, the bark of a tree etc. Use these for another observation game – 'Can you see what this is?'
- Look carefully together at activities in your setting and ask individual children to talk about their favourites.
- Let the children make a welcome book about their setting for new children starting the next term or year. Photograph favourite places and activities, and the places new children need to know about.
- Invite people who work in your setting, but not in your room, to come and talk to the children about their jobs.
- Collect some parts of games and other activities and play 'Can you put this back where it belongs?'
- Make a photo book of all the outdoor equipment in your setting and let children use it to talk about or select activities.
- Make up some songs about your setting, using familiar tunes e.g. 'We're going off to our school tomorrow' or 'Here we go off to school'.

Further questions and provocations

- What would happen if nobody cleaned our room?
- How does the manager know what things we need to play with and use? Where do they get them? (Don't forget to use catalogues and the Internet when children are finding the answers to these questions).
- Why do we need a lock on the front door?
- Who looks after the grass and plants in the garden?
- How could we change our nursery/school to make it look different?
- What do cleaners and premises officers do in the daytime, when they are not at our school?
- If we ordered a pizza from our nursery/school, how would they know where to bring it?
- What happens in our garden at night? What sort of animals and birds might come?
- How could we get birds or butterflies to come to our garden?
- Who locks the gates or the doors to keep our nursery/school safe? Who opens them and when do they do that? How do they make sure they don't forget?

Books and stories

- Starting School; Janet & Allan Ahlberg; Puffin
- Going to School; Anna Civardi; Usborne
- Curious George's First Day of School; Anna Grossnickle Hines; Houghton Mifflin

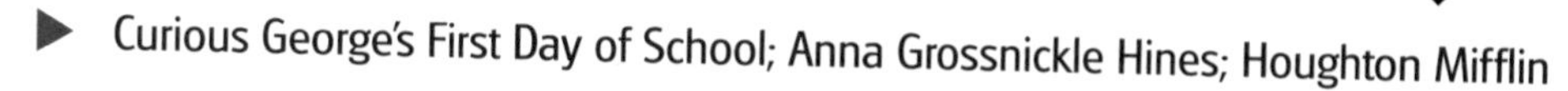

- Teacher's Pets; Dayle Ann Dodds; Candlewick
- My First Day at School; Rebecca Hunter; Evans
- Around a School; Sally Hewitt; Franklin Watts
- Going to School; Sally Hewitt; QED
- Going to Nursery; Laurence Anholt; Orchard
- My First day at Nursery School; Becky Edwards; Bloomsbury
- William and the Guinea Pig; Gill Rose; A & C Black, an imprint of Bloomsbury Publishing Plc

This exploration contributes to the following Goals for the EYFS:

PRIME

Communication and Language ① ③

Physical Development ① ②
PSED ① ② ③

SPECIFIC

Mathematics ① ②
Understanding of the World ① ② ③
Expressive arts and design ① ②

The exploration will also contribute to the Characteristics of Effective Learning:

Playing and exploring
Active learning
Creating and thinking critically

Explore your local park

What happens in a park? Focus: The local community

This investigation will involve several visits to your local park, in all seasons and weathers, looking at different things each time.

Talking time

Talk about your local park. Where is it? Who goes there? What goes on in the park? When do people go there?

As you talk, make an ideas map together and note what the children already know and what they want to find out. Here are some starter ideas for discussion – you will be able to think of more!

The first exploration:

- **Arrange a visit to your local park.** Make sure you follow your setting's Health and Safety policy for visits. Remember, it's always a good idea to visit yourself before taking children out.
- **You will need plenty of adults,** so check with parents to see who would like to come. Brief the parents before you go!
- **Check the places children will want to go, and the general layout** such as the play areas, and whether there are any animals such as ducks or squirrels to feed.
- **Make sure you know where the toilets are,** and see if there is a covered or protected area for snack, picnics or talk time, specially if it rains.
- **You could contact the Parks Department** and see if they can help with ideas for activities and things to see. They may also be happy to come and talk to the children about their work.
- **Talk about what you need to take,** and what you want to find out. Make a 'getting ready' list. This will be different if your visit is in winter or in summer, although you may need rain gear whatever the season! Here are some things the children might suggest, or you might consider taking:
  - Collecting bags for treasures
  - A snack or some drinks
  - Coats and suitable shoes or boots
  - Cameras
  - Some food for any animals or birds that live there
  - A ball or other games
  - A small first aid kit
  - Antiseptic spray or hand wipes

- **Talk about what you are going to see and do** when you are there. Children need to be prepared for the visit that may be different from the ones they take with their families. Here are some of the things you might suggest to look at:
  - The plants, trees and flowers growing in the park
  - The pitches and other games facilities

- The play area and other areas for children
- Water features, such as ponds and fountains
- Animals and birds that live in the park (some parks have mini zoos with birds or reptiles)

While you are there:

Most of the children will focus on the play area, so you might want to go there first, and if it is big enough, let them all have a turn on the apparatus.

Then spread yourselves out through the park, so you see everything. If different groups go to different parts of the park, at different times during the visit, they will have different information to bring back! This will provide a richer experience to share together, rather than everyone staying together.

Spend time talking with the children about what they can see in the park. Listen to their ideas about what they want to see, what they find, and what interests them. Let them choose where they want to go next.

Take as many cameras as you can and make sure that you and the children take lots of photos of the things they are interested in. Take photos of the children as well as the places and things you see.

Remember to visit the less obvious parts of the park, such as a bowling green, the place where the gardeners grow their plants, the trees and bushes etc. You may find some surprises such as a bandstand, a skateboarding park, a tree with flowers, or a seat with a good view. Make sure you explore these and talk about them too.

A snack or picnic makes the exploration even more fun, so make sure beforehand that everyone knows whether small groups will have their snack together or if the whole group will meet at an agreed time and place for a singsong and a game, as well as sharing what you have done and found.

When you get back you could:

- Make a collection of all the things you have found, and look at them together – sticks, leaves, small stones, feathers etc. Handle them, feel them, sort them, describe them, count them, arrange them, or draw them.

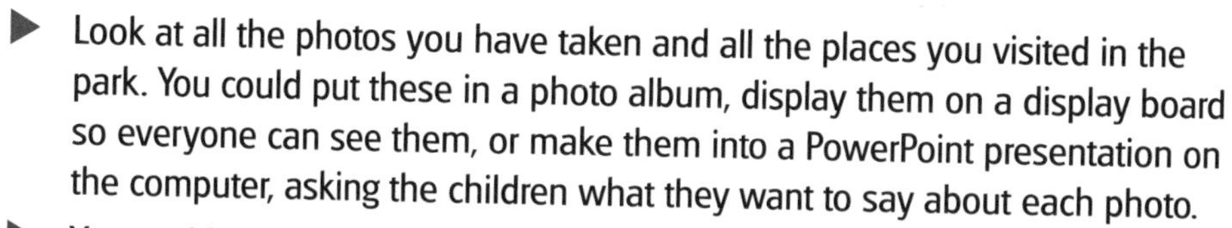

- Look at all the photos you have taken and all the places you visited in the park. You could put these in a photo album, display them on a display board so everyone can see them, or make them into a PowerPoint presentation on the computer, asking the children what they want to say about each photo.
- You could make a simple map on a very big piece of paper (or a shower curtain or piece of carpet). Draw pictures or stick photos of all the different places and things in the park, joining these by drawing paths and tracks between them, so the children can follow the way they went on the visit.
- As you talk about your local park you can ask some open questions about parks:
  - What do you like best about the park?
  - Are all parks the same as ours?
  - What could we do to make our park even better?
  - Is the park always the same?
  - What could you show your family when you go to the park next time?

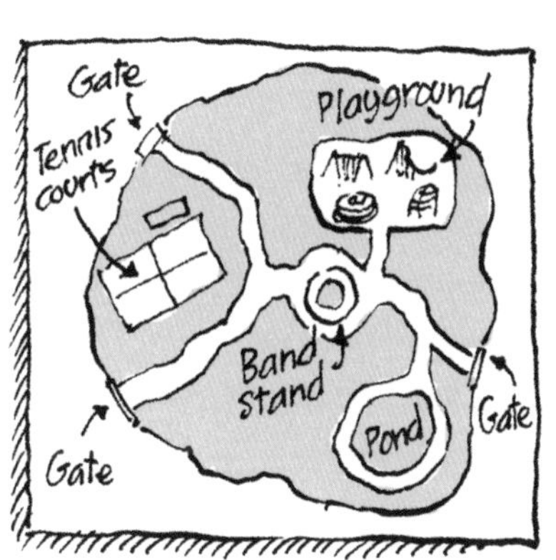

Some adult-initiated activities:

- Do some paintings of the park visit. You could suggest a collaborative painting or collage with all the children contributing ideas, pictures or textures for the background
- Introduce stories and rhymes about the park
- Use dance and dramatic play, based on activities during your visit
- Write thank you letters and draw pictures to send to the Parks Department.

Extensions into child-initiated learning (stimuli for children who are interested in replaying the experience):

- Provide Play people or Lego with playground equipment.
- Offer some equipment to make a role-play café or ice cream van, indoors or outside.
- Provide some wheelbarrows, badges and caps for park keeper play with wheeled toys.
- Offer some books or story tapes about parks (see booklist).
- Put your PowerPoint photo presentation of the park visit on the computer for free access.
- Record some songs with 'park based' words and let the children play these and record some more. An example might be 'We're all going to the park tomorrow' to the tune of 'Daddy's taking us to the zoo tomorrow.'

And together you could find out about parks by looking at or downloading some images from Google, or visiting some websites.

Google searches – park, park keeper, flower bed, park planting, tree planting, playground, farm park, zoo in the park, petting zoo, park in the dark, bandstand, skate park, ice cream van, park shelter, bowling green, tennis court, football pitch, floral display in park, fair, festival, flower show

Websites – http://www.rhs.org.uk – the Royal Horticultural Society where you can see pictures of flower shows and gardens

http://www.keepbritaintidy.org/GreenFlag is a site where you can find and vote for good parks in your area

http://www.dads-space.com/DaysOut is a site for Dads which give advice about play

http://www.royalparks.org.uk – where you can download a leaflet on London Parks

Enter your local town name and 'parks and gardens' in a search engine such as Google, and you should find a list of the parks in your area. Look in images for your local park to find photos and other information.

Work with puppets to explore events and possible problems arising in a park – falling over, getting lost, finding lost property and possible dangers (such as finding glass, needles, matches etc.) and decide what you would do in any of these situations.

Further experiences and visits to keep the interest alive:

- Visit your local park in different weathers and seasons such as:
  - An autumn visit to collect leaves, tree seeds and other natural objects
  - A winter (or even snowy) visit to look for changes to trees, plants, birds and animals
  - A spring visit to look for signs of new growth such as bulbs, new leaves and ducklings
- Contact your Parks Department and ask if you can come and watch grass mowing, flower planting or tree trimming.
- See if they have any spare plants when they have finished their planting. Could they come to your setting and help the children to plant them?
- Look in local papers for events such as carnivals, fairs, produce shows, flower shows etc. as well as sporting events. If you can't take the children, make sure you let parents know about interesting events that they might want to visit. Then the children can report back to you or build the experience into their play.
- Have a plant or flower show, or make miniature gardens on plates or in small bowls. See some pictures by Google Images 'miniature gardens' or http://www.oolamoola.co.uk/diy-tutorial-of-the-week-miniature-garden-centrepiece or http://www.cathkidston.co.uk/s-18-design-a-miniature-garden-competition.aspx for photos of all the entries in their recent miniature garden competition.
- Use recycled materials to make a miniature playground for small world characters with roundabouts, swings and slides made by the children.
- Make maps and pictures of your local park and send them to the Parks Department.
- Make a leaflet for parents about your local park. Use the children's pictures and photos, and let children take it home to inspire their families to visit their local park.

Further questions and provocations

- How could we make our outdoor area more interesting?
- Could we make a park or a playground for toys?
- What could we ask the park keepers to do to make the park safer?
- Why are parks good for children and their families?
- What would happen if we didn't have any parks?
- Who looks after the parks?
- Who pays for the parks?
- What are the dangerous things in the park?
- What grows in the park?
- Where do the park animals find food?
- What happens in the park at night?
- Who locks the gates? Who opens them and when do they do that? How do they make sure they don't forget?

Books and stories

- Park in the Dark; Martin Waddell; Walker Books
- After Dark in Acorn Park; Margaret McCaffrey; Legwork
- Voices in the Park; Anthony Browne; Corgi
- Shark in the Park; Nick Sharratt; Corgi
- Tales from Percy's Park (and other Percy the Park Keeper stories including seasonal stories and animal stories); Nick Butterworth; HarperCollins
- Spot Goes to the Park; Eric Hill; Warne
- Playing Outside: Activities, Ideas and Inspiration for the Early Years; Helen Bilton; David Fulton
- Nature and Young Children: Encouraging Creative Play and Learning in Natural Environments; Ruth Wilson; Routledge
- Parks and Gardens, Richard Spilsbury; Red Fox
- Playing in the Park; Jillian Powell; Franklin Watts
- Playgrounds (How do they work?); Wendy Sadler, Heinemann Children's Books
- In the Night Garden – a series of books to follow the series; BBC

This exploration contributes to the following Goals for the EYFS:

PRIME

Communication and Language (1) (3)
Physical Development (1) (2)
PSED (1) (2) (3)

SPECIFIC

Mathematics (1) (2)
Understanding of the World (1) (2) (3)
Expressive arts and design (1) (2)

The exploration will also contribute to the Characteristics of Effective Learning:

Playing and exploring

Active learning

Creating and thinking critically

Explore shopping

What happens in a shop? Focus: The local community

Before you start, you will need to find a friendly shop or supermarket to explore, preferably over several visits! The middle range or even smaller shops may be more welcoming, although a big superstore will have more space and probably more to look at.

Talking Time

Bringing a shopping list to your setting would be a good way to start the talk about shops and shopping. Talk about your list and where you need to go to get the things you need. The children may suggest you could get all your shopping in a supermarket, but some may have experience of smaller, more specialist shops such as bakers, butchers and chemists.

As you talk, note what the children say, what they already know and what they want to find out. You could make an ideas map about shops. Here are some starter ideas for discussion – you will be able to think of more!

The first exploration:

I will need

- **Arrange a visit to a supermarket or some shops.** Make sure you follow your setting's Health and Safety policy for visits. Remember, it's always a good idea to make a visit yourself before taking children out. Ask shopkeepers or the store manager to suggest a good time to bring children.
- **You will need plenty of adults**, so check with parents to see who would like to come. Brief the parents before you go. You may not be able to take all the children out at the same time, so you could plan a series of visits to different sorts of shops. Each group could be asked to buy something from a particular shop, for everyone to share or look at when they get back.
- **Talk about the shops you are going to visit.** You could introduce this visit by planning to do one of the following when you return, and making a list of what you need to buy:
  - Make sandwiches, with different sorts of bread and lots of different fillings
  - Have a small party with crisps, vegetable sticks, apple slices, juice and paper plates
  - Make soup with different sorts of vegetables
  - Write some letters, postcards or invitations, so you need paper, pens, envelopes and stamps
  - Make biscuits or a cake and ask the children to get the ingredients
  - Buy your own snacks and fruit for snack time.
- **To make the visit relevant to them**, give each small group an item to buy and some money to pay for it. Make mini-lists with pictures as well as the words of the objects they need to buy. Ask adult helpers to give the children as much responsibility as possible.
- **During this stage you could set up a role-play** shop in your setting. It's important to keep your home corner as well, the children need to leave a house and return with their shopping.
- **Ask the children what sort of shop they would like**, and what they need to make the shop. Look at the ideas map for suggestions of the sort of shop to make.

While you are there:

Encourage the children to ask questions, take photos and look carefully at what's in the shops. They probably don't have much time to look when they are with busy parents.

Remember what they have been asked to buy, and let them suggest where to get it. Let them decide if there are several choices, and explain how much money you have to buy the things on the list.

Take time to look at other things in the shop, or other shops if you are on a street. Some children never visit shops other than supermarkets so this may be a fascinating new experience for some of them.

Make a point of looking at unusual things, ones the children may not have seen. Take photos of these so you can talk about them later.

Talk to the shopkeepers, if they have time, and ask them about the things in their shop. Ask them if they mind having their photo taken by the children – most of them will be very willing!

When you are ready to pay, help the children to check their list, find the money and pay the shopkeeper or checkout person.

Make sure the children say 'Thank you' and 'Goodbye' to the shopkeepers before they leave.

Have a look at some more shops or other places as you walk back to your setting, taking photos of landmarks such as churches, post boxes, crossings and interesting gardens.

When you get back you could:

- Look together at the things you have bought.
- Look at all the photos you have taken at the shops. Print them out for the children to look at. They will be fascinated to see themselves in the shops, buying things, asking questions and looking at things. Having the photos in their hands will be very important to some children, so they can look really closely at what is happening, particularly if they haven't had their turn yet.
- Make a simple plan of the supermarket or a map of the street where the shops are, adding photos and asking children to draw themselves at the shops.
- As you talk about your shopping trip you can ask some open questions:
  - How did you get to the shops/supermarket?
  - What did you see on the way?
  - Did you see anything at the shops that you have never seen before?
  - What did you buy?
  - What did you photograph?
- If some children didn't go on this first visit, let them talk about what they were doing while you were away.

Some adult-initiated activities:

- Make maps and plans of the way to the shops.
- Look on Google Earth for aerial views of your setting or the shops.
- Read stories and sing songs about shopping (see book list).
- Plan some dance and dramatic play together, based on experiences during your visit.
- Work with puppets to discuss conversations and situations, particularly any the children found difficult, such as talking to adults they don't know.
- Talk with the children about the sort of shop they would like in their room. It doesn't have to be a food shop or supermarket; maybe they would like a clothes shop, a shoe shop or a sports shop?

- Help the children to make things for the role-play shop from playdough, clay or other materials, or to collect real objects to use.
- Take time to be in the role-play shop yourself, modelling and demonstrating the language and behaviour of shopping by playing alongside the children.
- Collect some purses, bags and baskets and talk about money – using real money (washed, small coins will do) makes the role-play much more realistic. You may also need to talk about credit and debit cards (and provide a machine in the role-play shop). Many children only see their parents pay with credit and debit cards.
- Collect shopping and mail order catalogues and junk mail, and add these to home role-play areas. Children love these and will spend time talking about them to others and to you.
- Play the memory game 'I went to the shops and I bought...'.

Extensions into child-initiated learning (stimuli for children who are interested in replaying the experience):

- Offer shopping trolleys in your outdoor area and include shopping bags, buggies and other shopping experiences indoors and outside
- Make resources available so children can make shops of their own – ice cream vans, pizza deliveries, perhaps even a fish and chip shop
- Offer some books or story tapes about shops and shopping (see booklist)
- Put a PowerPoint photo presentation of the shopping visit on the computer for free access
- Record some 'shopping' songs and provide a microphone for announcements.

And together you could find out about shops by looking at or downloading some images from Google, or visiting some websites.

Google searches – shop, supermarket, fruit, greengrocer, baker, cake shop, butcher, shoe shop, book shop (or any other shop the children want to see),

Websites – www.edupics.com/en-coloring-pictures-pages-photo-greengrocers-shop – has simple line drawings of different shopkeepers and what they sell.

Enter your local town name and 'supermarkets' in a search engine such as Google, and you should find a list of the supermarkets in your area. Enter other sorts of shops and find out where to see them. Then go and have a look!

Further questions and provocations

- How do the things get to the shops?
- Who pays the people who work in the shops?
- What happens to all the things that are left over?
- What are charity shops for?
- Where would I buy a wedding cake or a new pair of wellies?
- What would be a good name for a hat shop or a shop selling bikes?
- If you had a shop, what would you sell? What would you call your shop?
- What would we do if there were no shops?

Books and stories

- Where People Shop; Barbara Talyor; A & C Black, an imprint of Bloomsbury Publishing Plc
- The Shopping basket; John Burningham; Red Fox
- Don't Forget the Bacon; Pat Hutchins; Red Fox
- Going Shopping; Sarah Garland; Frances Lincoln
- The Great Pet Sale (book and CD); Mick Inkpen; Hodder
- The Runaway Shopping Cart; Kathy Long; Dutton
- Let's Go Shopping; Betty Moon; Collins Big Cat
- Shopping; Cassie Mayer; Heinemann
- Master Bun the Baker's Boy; Alan Ahlberg; Puffin
- Supermarket on Mars; Rigby Star
- Blue Glasses; Louise John; Wayland
- Going Shopping; Jillian Powell; Franklin Watts
- My Granny Went to Market; Stella Blackstone; Barefoot Books
- Markets; Cassie Mayer; Heinemann

This exploration contributes to the following Goals for the EYFS:

PRIME

Communication and Language ① ③

Physical Development ① ②

PSED ① ② ③

SPECIFIC

Mathematics ① ②

Understanding of the World ① ② ③

Expressive arts and design ① ②

The exploration will also contribute to the Characteristics of Effective Learning:

Playing and exploring

Active learning

Creating and thinking critically

Explore mud, stones and rocks

What is mud? Focus: The natural world

This exploration focuses on materials that have eternal fascination for children – mud, sand, gravel, soil, stones and rocks. You just need supplies of these and somewhere to explore them.

Talking time

This exploration is best if you start with some soil, compost or mud, and have a conversation while you play with them. If possible, have one adult working with the children while another records what you are all saying.

Talk about the materials as you play together. Ask some simple questions – What does it feel like, smell like, look like? What is mud made from? Where does it come from? What is it for?

As you talk, your colleague can note what the children say, what they already know and what they want to find out. Here are some starter ideas for discussion – you will be able to think of more!

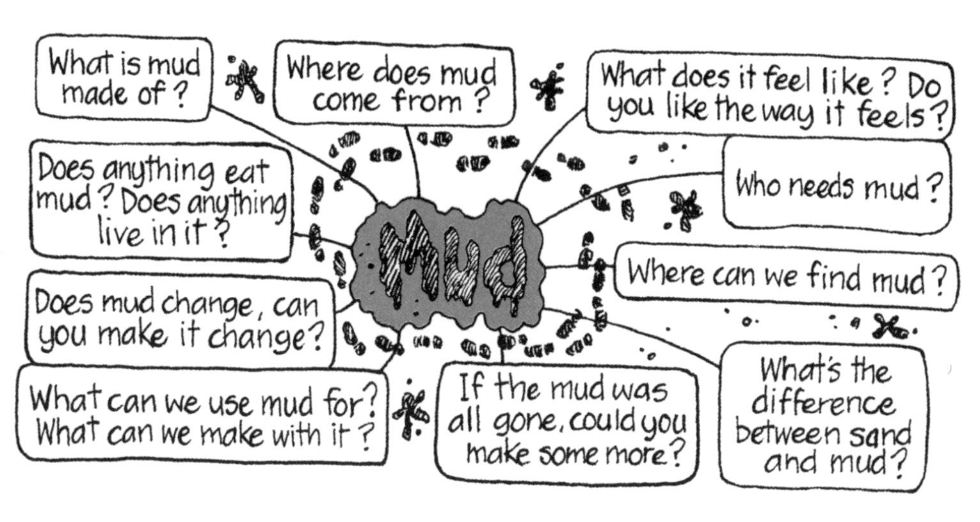

NOTE: You can use soil from a garden or buy a bag from a garden centre. The soil from a garden centre will be sterilised, so it is safer, but it's not as interesting because there will be no living things in it! If using garden soil, ensure children wash their hands carefully after the activities.

The first exploration:

I will need

- **Start with just mud**, compost, sand or gravel. It's easier to concentrate on one thing at a time.
- **Ask the children** 'If we're going to find out all about mud, what do you think we'll need? Make a list with the children, accept their ideas and add some of your own. Start collecting the resources together.
  - Tools for scooping, piling and transporting – spoons, spades, trowels, buckets
  - Tools and equipment for poking, trailing and drawing with mud – sticks, brushes, spoons, forks
  - Surfaces to make marks on – sheets, big sheets of card, walls and fences, shower curtains
  - Things to mix with the mud – water, gravel, sand, sequins
  - Clear plastic bottles and jars to mix samples of mud and water
  - Sieves and strainers
  - Magnifying glasses and small containers for samples
  - Toy diggers and trucks
  - Cameras, dictaphones, video cameras
- **As you start your explorations together, talk about** what you could do. Look at the tools and equipment you have collected, and name each one so the children know what they are called.
- **Make sure the children know about washing their hands** after playing with mud and soil, and not putting their fingers or tools in their mouths.
- **Take some photos** of them and note what they say as they work. They may want to add other things such as more water or stones.

While you are there:

Ask the children what they would like to do with the mud. Where and how would they like to work? Do they want to work indoors or outside, on a table or the floor?

Watch for things in the mud – worms, ants, spiders and other small creatures. Rescue these and return them to the garden after you have looked at them with magnifying glasses or in bug boxes.

Make sure you stay near the activity for at least for some of the time, to watch and listen to the conversations.

Now try adding more water to some of the mud so it is liquid enough to pour. See what the children can do with this runny mud. Ask them what they could use now. They may suggest brushes, jugs, tubes, sprays or funnels. Let them try each of the tools as they suggest them, and leave others where they can see them for inspiration.

Runny mud is good for:

- Painting on walls, paths and fences (let the children hose it off if it doesn't rain)
- Making pictures on big sheets of card, shower curtains or other big surfaces
- Spraying with hand sprayers
- Dripping and dropping
- Using with sponges for printing
- Pouring and tipping with jugs, tubing, funnels and guttering
- Adding paint to see what colours they can make.

When this new runny mud has been explored, try adding even more water and putting this in clear plastic bottles so the children can see what happens when the mud settles. It should form layers with sandy mud at the bottom and finer mud higher up. The water above this should be clear, with just bits of plant matter floating on the surface.

Look at these layers with magnifying glasses to see what they contain. Take photos to add to your 'Mud' book or picture collection.

Ask the children if they can get the water out of wet mud.

Experiment with their suggestions – take them seriously and try them all. Look at the dry mud you get from the wet mixture and talk about where the water has gone.

After your first exploration:

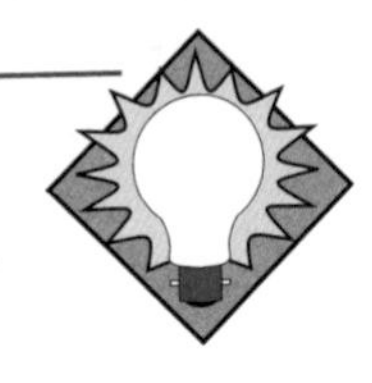

When the children have finished exploring mud, you could offer another sort of material alongside the mud, in a different container. You could try:

- damp sand
- gravel (pea gravel is rounded and nicer to play with)
- vermiculite
- decorative stone
- grey or red clay.

As you add these new materials, let the children explore them and compare how they look, feel, smell and behave when handled.

You could put a handful of each in the middle of a piece of card and write all the words the children use to describe it round the edge. Take a photo of these and use them as talking points, either printed out or on the computer.

Some adult-initiated activities:

- Show the children how to make simple shakers by putting small amounts of sand, gravel or stones in small water bottles and taping the tops on with duct tape.
- Make underwater bottle gardens by putting sand or coloured gravel in the bottom of bigger water bottles and adding water, blue colouring and small plastic fish and plants cut from coloured plastic carrier bags.
- Use clay to make simple sculptures or just for free play. If you can get some air-drying clay, children will enjoy keeping their creations.
- Roll out some clay and use tools to poke holes and make patterns. Push beads, sequins and other small items into rolled clay, add paint or glitter and leave to dry. If you make a hole right through the clay, you can hang the creations up.

Extensions into child-initiated learning (stimuli for children who are interested in replaying the experience):

- Offer stones, twigs, logs and branches to add to the mud and gravel as a change from commercial tools.
- Offer a choice of different small world characters and vehicles – people, diggers, dinosaurs, superheroes etc.
- Add some guttering and drainpipes to a big tray of sand or gravel for making tunnels and holes. Children may then like to pour water down these or drive vehicles through them.
- Add some hard hats, barrows and spades for shifting gravel and stones round the outside area.
- Help the children make their own picture stories using cameras and DVD and play these on the computer or burn them onto CD to take home.
- Make environments for plastic bugs and spiders.
- Offer a big tray of mud for footprints with boots or bare feet.

And together you could find out about mud, sand and gravel by looking at or downloading some images from Google, or visiting some websites.

Google searches – mud, muddy, soil, compost, clay, rain, puddle, ploughing, digging, mud bank, school gardens

If you Google 'mud pies' you will also get links to recipes for edible Mud Pies that are simple enough for the children to make.

Websites – www.soilassociation.org, www.thegrowingschoolsgarden.org.uk, http://apps.rhs.org.uk/schoolgardening all have guidance on growing your own plants in a school garden.
http://www.parentingscience.com/preschool-science-projects-dirt.html has simple experiments for children

http://www.ecofriendlykids.co.uk/celebrating-earth-day.html gives information about celebrating Earth Day

Further questions and provocations

- Where does the water in puddles go?
- How do we know about dinosaurs from their footprints?
- What would happen if it didn't rain again?
- Why do some beaches have sand and some have gravel or stones?
- Could you make your own sand from stones?
- Can plants grow in sand or gravel?
- Why does gravel make a noise when you walk on it?
- Is wet sand or dry sand better for sandcastles? Can you make a sandcastle with gravel? Why not?

Books and stories

- Mudworks; Maryanne F Kohl; Bright Ring
- We're Going on a Bear Hunt; Michael Rosen, Walker
- One Duck Stuck; Phyllis Root; Walker Books
- Mr Gumpy's Outing, John Burningham; Red Fox
- Mrs Wishy Washy; Joy Cowley; Philomel

- Mrs Wishy Washy; Joy Cowley; Philomel
- Alfie's Feet; Shirley Hughes; Red Fox
- Wiggling Worms; Wendy Pfeffer; Harper Trophy
- Diary of a Worm, Doreen Cronin; HarperCollins
- What's Underground?; Gill Munton; Collins Big Cat
- Eddie's Garden, How to make things grow; Sarah Garland; Frances Lincoln
- How a Seed Grows; Helene Gordon; Collins
- A Seed in Need; Sam Godwin; Wayland
- The Little Book of Growing Things; Sally Featherstone; Featherstone, an imprint of Bloomsbury Publishing Plc
- The Little Book of Clay and Malleable Materials; Lorraine Frankish; Featherstone, an imprint of Bloomsbury Publishing Plc
- Clay; Mary Firestone; Capstone

This exploration contributes to the following Goals for the EYFS:

PRIME

Communication and Language (1)(3)
Physical Development (1)(2)
PSED (1)(2)(3)

SPECIFIC

Mathematics (1)(2)
Understanding of the World (1)(2)(3)
Expressive arts and design (1)(2)

The exploration will also contribute to the Characteristics of Effective Learning:

Playing and exploring

Active learning

Creating and thinking critically

Explore houses and homes

Where do people and animals live? Focus: The local community

An exploration of houses and homes can expand to cover homes anywhere, not just houses for people, but animal, bird and insect homes, and even underwater homes. You may want to use this longer exploration as an alternative to the more usual topics 'All About Me' or 'My Home'.

Talking time

Start this exploration by talking about where the children live. Do they live in a house, a flat or a terrace or a semi? And which other homes have they visited? Talk about grandparents, friends, holiday homes, tents and caravans.

As you talk, make an ideas map together and note what the children already know and what they want to find out. Here are some starter ideas for discussion – you will be able to think of more!

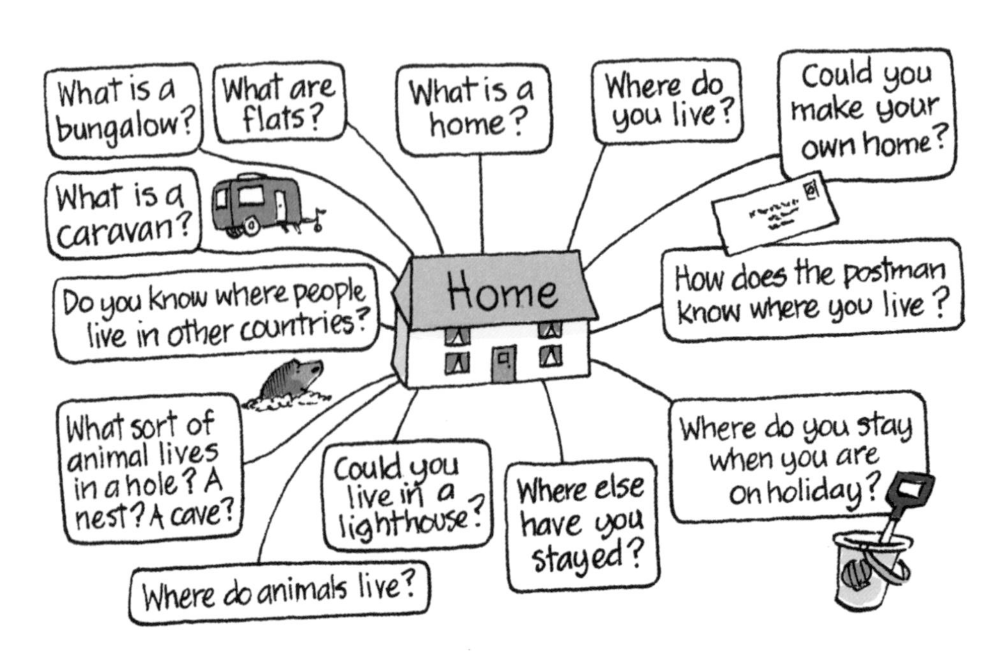

The first exploration:

- **Go out in your local community.** Look at the houses you see there. Take some photos and do some drawings. If possible, visit the streets where the children live.
- **Lend parents some cameras to take photos** of their own homes, both outside and indoors. These will make a great book.
- **Talk about what you need to take** on your walk and what you want to find out. Make a 'getting ready' list. Here are some things the children might suggest, or you might consider taking:
  - Cameras
  - A local street map
  - A bag for leaflets and information
  - Clipboards or whiteboards for drawing
  - A dictaphone
  - A small first aid kit

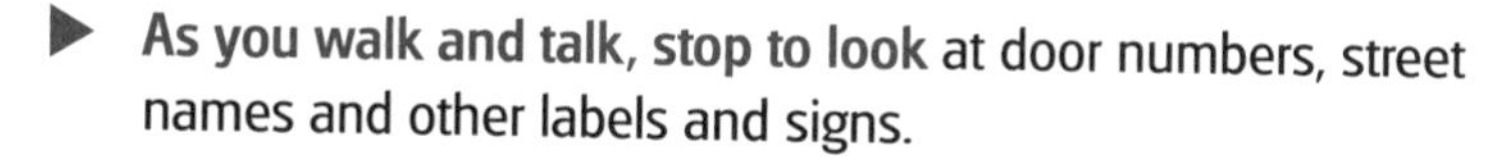

While you are there:

- **As you walk and talk, stop to look** at door numbers, street names and other labels and signs.
- **Keep your eyes open** for different sorts of houses and homes.
- **Look at different kinds** of windows, doors and chimneys.
- **Look at the patterns** on walls and roofs.
- **Visit some estate agents** and collect some information about homes in your local area.

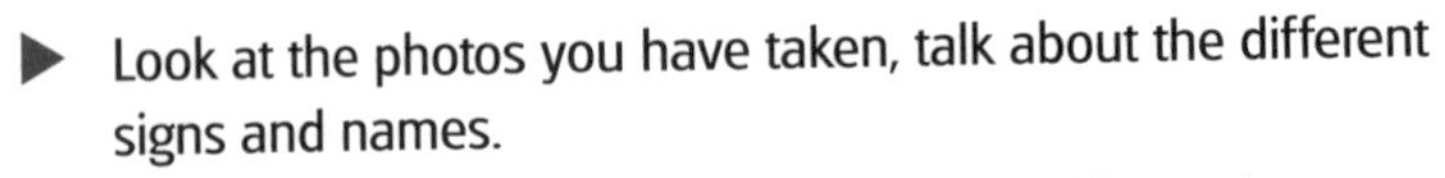

When you get back you could:

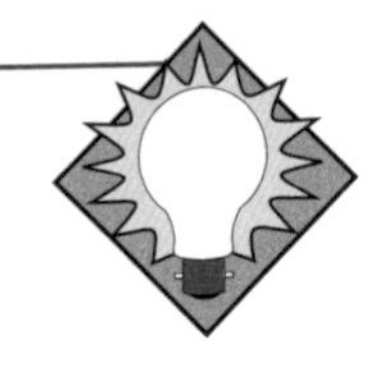

- Look at the photos you have taken, talk about the different signs and names.
- Discuss houses with names and houses with numbers.
- Use some non-fiction books to look at different sorts of houses and other buildings.
- Look at local newspapers to see what sorts of houses are popular in the area, and some unusual places and unusual homes, care homes, flats, apartments over shops and offices, older houses with big gardens and gates, even a castle or a houseboat.

Find out about homes by looking at or downloading some images from Google, or visiting some websites

Google searches – home, house, holiday home, build a house, tent, hut, igloo, shelter, lighthouse, castle, houseboat, postman, post box, letters, envelope, parcel, nest, burrow, hole, cave

Websites – www.ukstockimages.com/catsearch/Postman.htm has royalty free post office photos

http://www.freemaptools.com/uk-postcode-map.htm is a postcode map where you can plot your own postcode

http://www.streetmap.co.uk is a map site where you can see your own street, town, setting or school.

http://www.caravanclub.co.uk for pictures and information

http://www.tentastic.co.uk a good tent site

http://www.bbc.co.uk/nature/animals/wildbritain/field_guides/animal_homes.shtml has pictures of animal homes.

http://www.bbc.co.uk/cbbc/wild/ has animals and animal games to play

Exploring their own homes:

You will need the help of parents for some of these activities – others can be done by the children from memory:

- Ask parents to help their children to photograph their own front doors and use these to make a pop-up book called 'Who lives here?' Print the door photos and stick each door by the left hand edge to a piece of card, so it can open and close. Now take a photo of each child, print them and let the children stick them behind their own door. Punch holes in each card and use ribbon or tape to fix the pages together. Make a cover and your book is done. Children will love it!
- Find some pictures of castles, caves, caravans, palaces, spooky buildings or houseboats. Stick them onto card so they can stand up. Make small stick puppets with photos of the children or other characters and use these as puppets to look out of the windows and doors of the different buildings.
- Together, make a simple map of your local area on a very big piece of paper. Draw pictures or stick on photos of all the houses, homes and other buildings in your area. Don't worry about scale or accuracy; this is just to get the concept of a map.
- Get a street map (or an aerial photo) of the area round your setting and help the children to find their houses. Google Earth is a good way to find aerial maps. Just put the postcode of your setting in Google Maps and you can enlarge the picture so you can see individual houses from the air. Print these and enlarge them on a photocopier. Display the photos and let the children talk about them, finding their own homes and looking at their community from the air.

Some adult-initiated activities:

- Either take photos of houses or ask children to bring a photo of their own house. Use these for naming parts of a house (such as window, door, garage, chimney, porch) or for comparing houses and finding differences between them.
- Ask children to talk about the place they like best in their house and describe what it is like.
- Offer very big cardboard boxes for making houses. Help the children to cut out doors and windows. Let them paint and decorate them as they like.

Extensions into child-initiated learning (stimuli for children who are interested in replaying the experience):

- Offer Play people or Lego characters with a home-made or commercial doll's house. Don't forget homes for popular characters from film and TV too, such as Batman's cave, Ben Ten's mobile home, and Barbie's caravan, etc.
- Provide materials for making their own houses for soft toys or small world people.
- Provide plenty of den making materials, canes, net curtains, plastic sheeting, clothes pegs, elastic bands, duct tape, masking tape, cable ties etc. so children can make their own dens and shelters.
- If the children get interested in den-making, find out about dens and shelters by looking at or downloading some images from Google, or visiting some websites:

Google searches – den, treehouse, forest den, willow den, stick den, cane den, forest school den, shelter, kid's shelter, shelter building, tent, tepee, kid's tepee, do-it-yourself kid's tepee

Websites – http://www.forestry.gov.uk/forestry (forestry commission den building guidance); www.goingwild.net; www.mindstretchers.co.uk (resources and den making kits); www.woodlandtrust.org.uk; www.muddyfaces.co.uk (den-building equipment); http://www.forestschools.com (the home site for Forest Schools)

- Offer camping and holiday equipment such as picnic plates and cutlery, camping kettles and pans, enamel bowls and water carriers.
- Provide some pop-up tents for creative play where children who are not so interested in building can quickly make a house and start playing.
- Read stories and look at non-fiction books about houses and homes.

Further experiences and visits to keep the interest alive:

- Offer some more challenging den-making equipment – tent pegs and mallets, string, branches and logs, groundsheets, plastic sheeting or black bin liners. Help children to learn joining techniques and different ways of making their structures stand up.

- Find a local building site and watch the builders at work (you won't be able to go onto the site, but you can often see from behind a fence). If there isn't a suitable building site nearby, get a copy of 'What if we were Builders', Featherstone's resource pack of photos, print materials, and a photographic PowerPoint presentation, of builders making a house.

- Look at homes for pets. Explore cages, kennels, fish bowls and other homes for cats, dogs, goldfish, rabbits and guinea pigs. See if you can find a pet shop to visit if you can't borrow some pets from families in your setting.

- Talk about where storybook characters live. Tell the stories of The Three Little Pigs, The Three Bears, Hansel and Gretel or other traditional tales where there are story book houses to talk about.

- Try doing some building with real bricks. Children will love the weight and sound of real bricks. Remember to warn them about the difference between wooden and real bricks!

- Ask an architect or builder to come to your setting to talk to the children about their work. If they can bring hard hats and plans, so much the better.

- Make simple zigzag books of their own houses, with a page for each room and some of their favourite things.

- Offer unusual materials to make miniature shelters and homes for toys and animals – straw, twigs and sticks, hay and drinking straws. Older children could use fabric, bubble wrap or plastic sheeting to make their dens waterproof or private.

- Use their dens as spaces to read stories, sing songs or just be together. You could offer some sleeping bags, to snuggle into in their dens, as they read or sing.

Further questions and provocations

- Why do some people live in flats?
- How does the postman find your house?
- Why do we have different names for streets?
- What is best about your bedroom?
- If you could move, where would you live?
- What does a builder use a crane for?
- What sticks bricks together?
- Where do elephants and crocodiles sleep?
- Could you live in a tree?
- Who lives in a cave?
- What lives in a spooky house?
- Do you know any songs or rhymes about houses and building?

Books and stories

- Handa's Surprise; Eileen Browne; Walker Books
- On the Way Home; Jill Murphy; MacMillan
- Come Home with Us; Annie Kluber; Child's Play
- Houses and Homes; Ann Morris; William Morrow
- Home; Kate Petty; Frances Lincoln
- The Little Topic Book of Where We Live; Featherstone, an imprint of Bloomsbury Publishing Plc
- Moving House; Anne Civardi; Usborne
- A Dark Dark Tale; Ruth Brown; Red Fox
- What's in the Witch's Kitchen? Nick Sharratt; Walker Books
- Animal Homes; Judy Tatchell; Usborne
- Squirrels and their Nests (one of a series); M Rustad; Capstone
- In The Castle; Anna Milbourne; Usborne

- What if We Were Builders? (CD and other resources); Featherstone, an imprint of Bloomsbury Publishing Plc
- Rosie and Jim stories
- Nature's Playground; Fiona Danks & Jo Schofield; Frances Lincoln
- Baby and Beyond, Dens and Shelters; Sally Featherstone; Featherstone, an imprint of Bloomsbury Publishing Plc
- A Den is a Bed for a Bear; Becky Baines; National Geographic Society
- The Best Den Ever; Ann Cassidy; Franklin Watts
- Sally's Secret, Shirley Hughes; Red Fox
- My Camp-Out; Marcia Leonard; Millbrook

This exploration contributes to the following Goals for the EYFS:

PRIME

Communication and Language 
Physical Development ① ②
PSED ①②③

SPECIFIC

Mathematics ① ②
Understanding of the World ① ② ③
Expressive arts and design ① ②

The exploration will also contribute to the Characteristics of Effective Learning:

Playing and exploring
Active learning
Creating and thinking critically

Explore a wood

How do trees grow from such tiny seeds? Focus: The natural world

For this exploration, you will need to have access to a local woodland, a wooded area in your school grounds, a local park, or a country park where you have access to a group of trees.

Talking time

Talk about woods and trees. Why do people like woods and trees? Who works in a wood? What sorts of animas live there? Have any of the children been to a wood or forest? What was it like?

As you talk, make an ideas map together and note what the children already know and what they want to find out. Here are some starter ideas for discussion – you will be able to think of more!

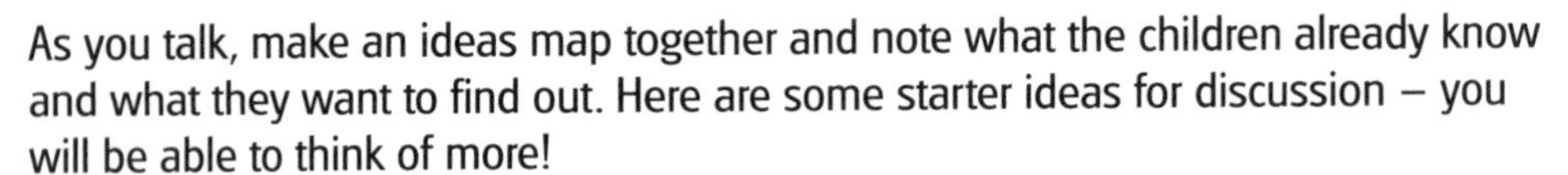

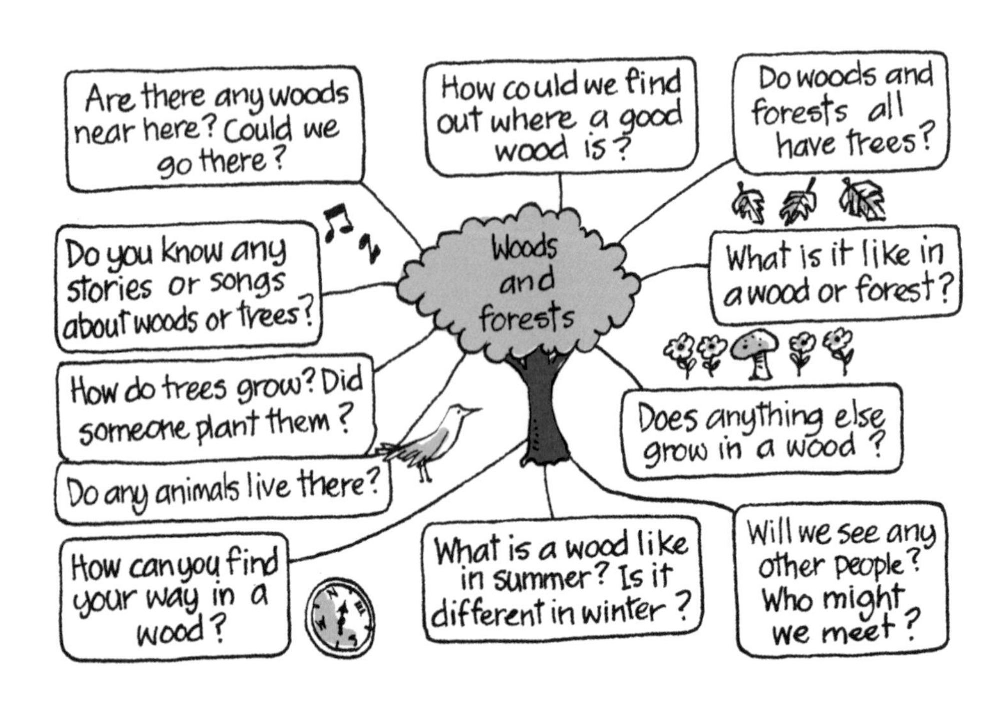

The first exploration:

I will need

- **Research your local area** and find a suitable wood for your group to visit. You should visit this area before you take the children, and follow your setting's Health and Safety policy.
- **Arrange a visit for your group**. You will need plenty of adults, so check with parents to see who would like to come. Brief the parents before you go!
- **You could contact the Forestry or Woodland managers** and ask them for help and guidance on bringing young children to the woods. They may be able to help you and may even offer to come with you on your woodland walk, or help with ideas for activities and things to see. They may also be happy to come and talk to the children about their work.
- **Think carefully about where you will take the children**. If it's a new place for you, everyone should stay close together so children and helpers feel safe on this first visit. Most managed woodlands provide maps and some have marked paths and routes.
- **Make sure you know where the toilets are** and locate a good place for a snack or picnic time, and a place to meet if you get separated or decide to do different things.
- **Before you go**, talk about what you are going to see and do when you are there. Here are some of the things you might explore:
  - Holes and nests
  - Trees and bushes
  - Plants and flowers
  - Birds and insects
  - Tracks and footprints.
- **Talk about what you need to take**, and what you want to find out. Make a 'getting ready' list. Take into account the season and the weather. Remember that it is often cooler under trees, so children should bring coats as well as strong shoes. Here are some things the children might suggest, or you might consider taking:
  - Collecting bags for treasures, or short pieces of wool for 'collection sticks'
  - Large bin bags to sit on if the ground is damp

- A snack or picnic and drinks
- Bags or small rucksacks/backpacks
- Coats and suitable shoes or boots
- Cameras and a Dictaphone or simple recorder to record sounds
- Binoculars and 'bug collectors' – boxes for observing minibeasts
- A small first aid kit
- Whistles are useful for calling each other
- Antiseptic spray or hand wipes.

While you are there:

This visit may involve a bus or minibus journey. Make this part of the visit by looking for directions and items of interest. If you are walking, use the opportunity to practise road safety and local knowledge of the area.

When you get to the woods, spend time making sure the adults and children know about staying close. (Encourage them to stay where they can see you, not where you can see them!) Talk about listening to adult instructions and directions. Make sure children know which adult is leading their group.

Remind everyone that they should NOT pick living plants, flowers or leaves, but they can collect things they find on the ground (seeds, stones, sticks, fallen leaves). Show them how to make a treasure collection by finding their own stick and winding some wool round leaves, feathers, twigs and other things they find.

Take as many cameras as you can find and make sure that you and the children take lots of photos of the things they are interested in. Take photos of the children as well as places and things. Ask the adults to take some photos of the trees and leaves, flowers and plants, so you have a good selection when you get back. Use the bug collectors to look at insects you find by gently moving stones and logs to look underneath, ensuring you put them back where you found them after you have looked at them.

As you explore the woods, remind the children to listen carefully and move quietly (at least some of the time) so they can see and hear the sounds of the woods.

When you stop for a snack or picnic, you could sit on a fallen log, a grassy slope or just by the path. Ask the children what they have found out about woods and trees, using some of the questions and answers from your ideas map and other conversations.

Before you leave, encourage the children to check their collections and have a last look at the place so they can remember where they have been.
Remember to take your litter home with you!

When you get back you could:

- Make a simple map on a big piece of paper, card or carpet. Draw pictures or stick photos of all the different places you found in the woods, adding the paths and picnic spots, so the children can revisit their walk by tracing the way they went.
- Look at all the things you have found – treasure sticks, leaves, stones, feathers, tree seeds etc. Name them, feel them, sort them, describe them, count them, arrange them, or draw them. Look at any tree seeds you have found and find out what sort of trees they will grow into.
- Download the photos you took onto your computer and look at them together. Let the children choose whether to put them in a photo album, display them on the wall, or make them into a PowerPoint presentation with the children's own words about the woodland adventure.
- If you recorded some sounds, listen to them and see if you can remember what made them.
- As you talk about your woodland walk ask some open questions:
  - Which part of the walk did you like best?
  - How tall were the trees?
  - Why was it darker in the woods?
  - Would the woods be the same if we went back at night? What would be different?
  - What sorts of animals and insects did we see?
  - Can we put some more ideas or pictures on our ideas map?

Some adult-initiated activities:

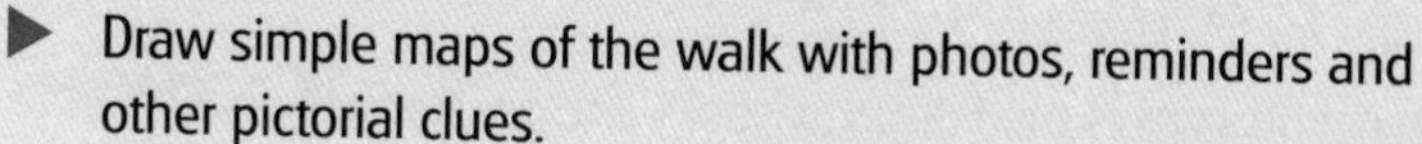

- Draw simple maps of the walk with photos, reminders and other pictorial clues.

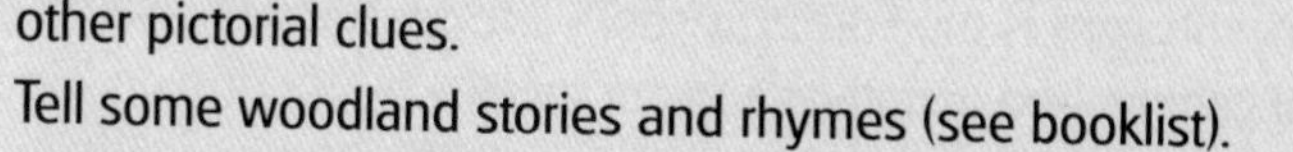

- Tell some woodland stories and rhymes (see booklist).

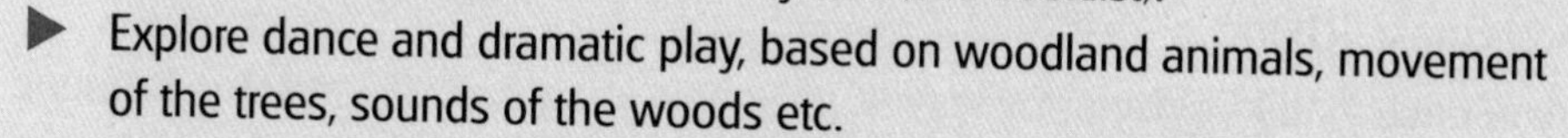

- Explore dance and dramatic play, based on woodland animals, movement of the trees, sounds of the woods etc.
- Talk about growth and how such big trees can grow from such small seeds. Look at some seeds together if you can – acorns, conkers, beech nuts, sycamore 'helicopters'.

Extensions into child-initiated learning (stimuli for children who are interested in replaying the experience):

- Provide stones, twigs, logs and branches for construction as a change from commercial sets.
- Collect different sorts of leaves to sort, draw, count and print with.
- Parks and forestry companies will often let schools and nurseries have logs and tree slices for outdoor construction or seats.
- Provide some books or story CDs about woods (see booklist).
- Offer free access to the photos so children can make their own books or presentations.
- Fill some plastic trays with soil or compost and provide sticks, twigs and other natural materials for making woodland environments for animals and play people.

And together you could find out about trees and woods by looking at or downloading some images from Google, or visiting some websites.

Google searches – tree, trees, forest, Forest School, tall trees, woodland, woodland walk, children in woods, leaves, tree seeds, acorn/conker/seed growing, biggest tree, bonsai

Websites – http://www.british-trees.com - the Woodland Trust - tree pictures and lots of free charts, pictures & ideas for activities for children in the Nature Detectives section http://www.treecouncil.org.uk the Tree Council – ideas, walks and events

http://www-saps.plantsci.cam.ac.uk/trees/index.htm is a brilliant, easy to use tree identification website for UK species.

http://www.forestschools.com is the Forest School website. You will also be able to find Forest School centres and initiatives in your locality by clicking on 'Find your local Forest School'.

If you enter 'Andy Goldsworthy leaves' in Google images you'll get some inspiring pictures of an artist who uses natural materials to make patterns and pictures.

Further experiences and visits to keep the interest alive:

- Visit your woods in different seasons. Collect seeds and leaves in autumn, look up at the bare branches in winter, hunt for bluebells and frogspawn in spring or go for a summer picnic.
- Go back to the woods and look very closely at bark, leaves, seeds and buds. Take photos, rubbings and prints of tree textures. Find trees with smooth and rough bark.
- Go back for a special minibeast hunt. Collect some minibeasts and take photos or draw them. Don't forget to put them back where you found them!
- Collect leaves, twigs and other objects to make some patterns in your outdoor area (Andy Goldsworthy).
- Make trees from construction materials, clay, collage or other materials. Look for some ideas in the guide 'Learning, Playing and Interacting' (DCSF 2009).

- Get some pots and compost and plant acorns, conkers and any other tree seeds you can find. Tree seeds grow slowly, so put them somewhere cool and shady and leave them until next spring when you may get a surprise! When they are too big for the pots, plant the baby trees in your garden area or back in their own wood where you can visit them.
- Look for local information on tree planting projects and see if you can join in. They may give you some trees to plant in your own setting or school. Encourage parents to get involved in tree planting with you.
- Keep children's interest in trees and woods alive throughout the year by looking at trees in your outdoor area, in local gardens, parks and playgrounds.
- Plant some apple pips and see if you can grow an apple tree. You may want to buy a container-grown one from a garden centre to watch while you wait.
- Keep on watching bugs, beetles, butterflies and other insects by leaving some logs in the play area as a habitat. Lift these gently from time to time to see what has come to live there.

Further questions and provocations

- What do trees need to make them grow?
- Why do the leaves fall off some trees in the winter?
- Do all trees lose their leaves in winter?
- Trees are so tall, why don't they fall over?
- Why do we need trees? What do we use them for?
- How can you tell how old a tree is?
- Do trees have flowers?
- What sorts of animals and other creatures live in trees?
- Could a tree go on growing till it reached the sky?

Books and stories

- The Great Kapok Tree; Lynn Cherry; Harcourt
- In the Dark, Dark Wood; Jessica Souhami; Frances Lincoln
- Spot's Walk in the Woods; Eric Hill; Puffin
- The Foggy Foggy Forest; Nick Sharratt; Walker Books
- An Oak Tree's Life; Nancy Dickmann; Heinemann
- From Seed to Apple Tree; Suzanne Slade; Picture Window
- Tales from Percy's Park; Nick Butterworth; HarperCollins
- Ferdie and the Falling Leaves; Julia Rawlinson; Gullane
- Seeds, Trees and Flowers; Rhonda Vansant; TAB Books
- Why do Leaves Change Colour? Betsy Maestro; Collins
- Autumn Nature Activities for Children; Bregitte Walden; Floris (a series, with a book for each season)
- Nature's Playground; Fiona Danks; Francis Lincoln

This exploration contributes to the following Goals for the EYFS:

PRIME

Communication and Language ① ③
Physical Development ① ②
PSED ① ② ③

SPECIFIC

Mathematics ① ②
Understanding of the World ① ② ③
Expressive arts and design ① ②

The exploration will also contribute to the Characteristics of Effective Learning:

Playing and exploring

Active learning

Creating and thinking critically

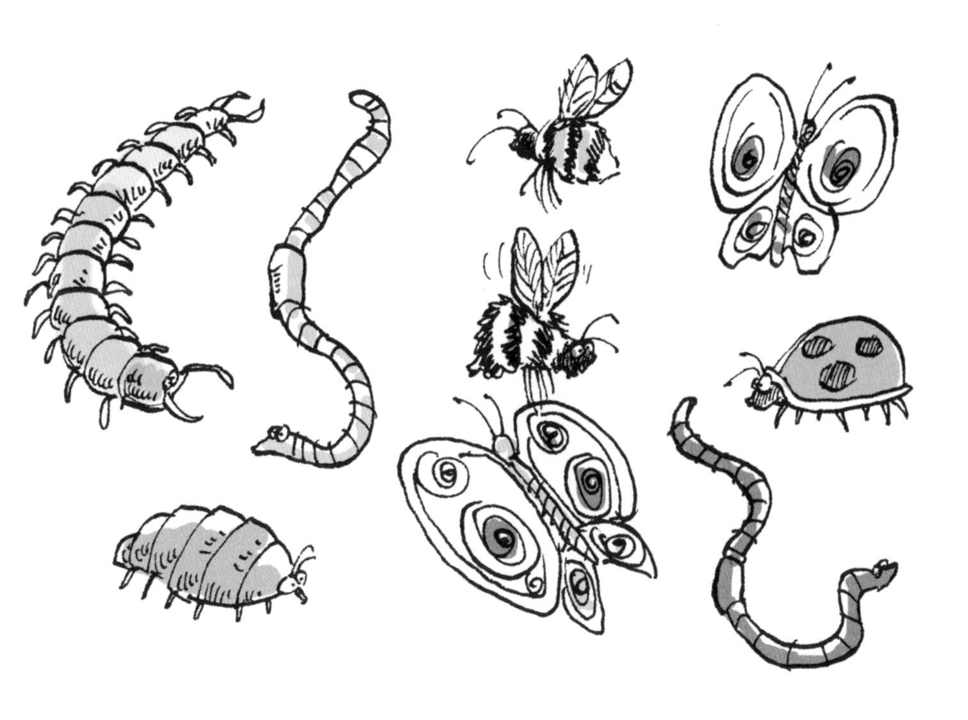

Explore colour, pattern and shape

How many colours and shapes are there in the world? Focus: Changes

This investigation is a good long-term one to use as a background to your work over a whole term or even longer. We suggest you start with colour, perhaps using a collection of objects of simple single colours (buttons, plastic toys, counters, big beads); and deal with pattern and shape in later parts of your exploration.

Talking time

Talk about colours. Ask some questions about colour and confirm what children already know.

As you talk, make an ideas map together and note what the children know and what they might want to explore. Here are some starter ideas for discussion – you will be able to think of more!

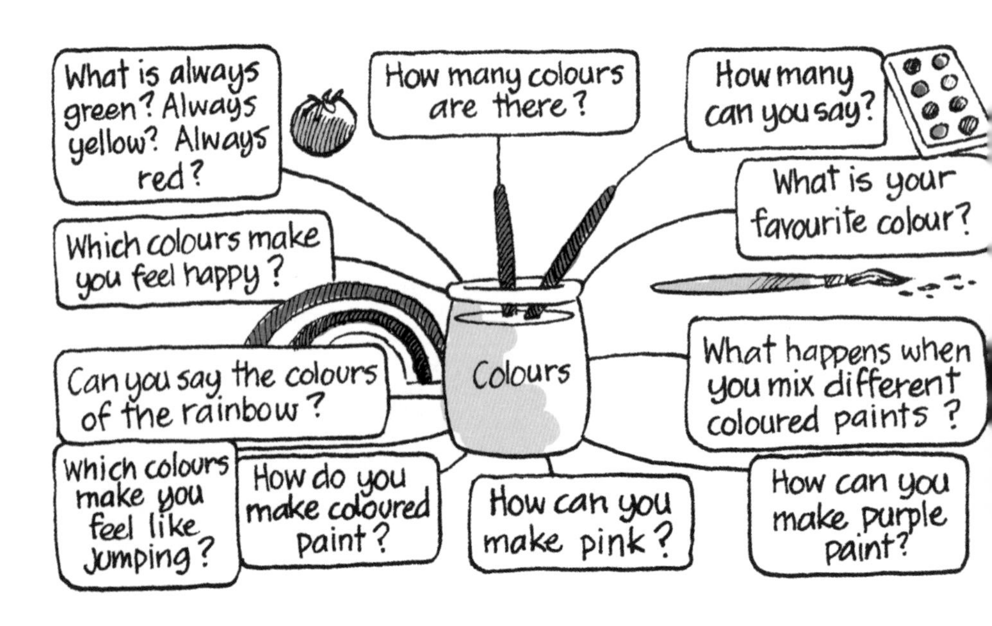

The first exploration:

- **Go on a colour walk** around your setting, your garden or your local community. Take a camera with you and take photos of the colours you see. Don't forget to look up and down, and collect some of the more unusual colours such as grey, brown and black. Make sure you follow your setting's Health and Safety policy for visits.
- **Take as many adults as you can**, to encourage the children to talk, so check with parents to see who would like to come.
- **Here are some places** the children might look for colours:
  - In the grass
  - Under bushes and trees
  - In reflections such as windows and puddles
  - In trees and in the sky
  - On paths, pavements, roads
  - In shop windows
  - On clothing
  - On vehicles
  - On doors, windows, curtains
  - Under logs and seats, behind cupboards
  - In signs, logos and adverts.
- **Some tips for a colour walk**
  - Take close-up photos of things like the yellow lines on the road, a red garden gate or the surface of a leaf.
  - Photograph parts of things, a door frame, a close-up of a coat button.
  - Look for unusual colours, shades and tones.
  - If you are in the garden or park, you could collect objects of different colours to bring back.

When you get back you could:

- Talk about the colours you have seen, giving the children plenty of time to think about what they saw.
- Download your photos and look at these. Print some out so the children can handle them. Sort the photos into colour collections and add some objects from around your room.
- Make some colour baskets for the colours you have found and encourage children to add to them over the next few days. In group time, use these baskets for sorting or discussion.

Some adult-initiated activities:

- Tear out colours from the pictures in catalogues and magazines. Sort these and look at shades and tones.
- Make some coloured ribbon sticks or find some coloured chiffon scarves and do a colour dance as you wave them.
- Give each child a small paint shade card (from DIY stores) and see if they can find something to match each of the shades or colours. Green shades are good for hunting among leaves and grasses.
- Make some group patchwork pictures with scraps and squares of pictures or fabrics sorted into colour groups.
- Make a big tie-dye drape from an old sheet. Tie stones or other objects into the fabric, using elastic bands. Then dye the whole sheet. Let it dry; remove the bands to see a great pattern. If you like, you can see what happens when you tie the stones in different places and dye the sheet again with a different colour.
- Let children work in pairs to put washing up liquid or flour in the paint and predict what they think will happen as they mix it.
- Play rhyming 'I spy something... ' with colours, using these lines:

  I spy something green, can you see what I have seen?
  I spy something red, can you see what I have said?
  I spy something blue, look and you will see it too.
  I spy something pink, this will really make you think.
  I spy something brown, look all round, look up and down.

Extensions into child-initiated learning (stimuli for children who are interested in replaying the experience):

- After a walk or other visit, talk about the colours you have seen. Help the children to mix these colours and shades to use in their paintings.
- Draw on damp paper with felt pens and watch the colours mix and new ones appear.
- Use hand sprays and diluted food colouring to spray on big sheets of paper. Watch how the drips mix and the colours merge.
- Make charts of favourite colours, using squares of the colours, or a square sponge for each count.
- Use droppers to drop food colouring into big jars of water or onto sheets of damp paper.
- Mix bright paint colours with icing sugar and use this to paint with. See what happens to the colours.
- When using powder paint, adding the water can be a problem. Provide the children with plastic pipettes so they can get the amounts right. Adding a tiny drop of washing up liquid will help powder paint to mix.
- Help the children to persevere with mixing and don't be tempted to take over. They will learn more if they do it themselves!

Further experiences to keep the interest alive:

- Talk about making and mixing colours, and make a list with the children, accepting their ideas and collecting the resources together.
  - Colour charts from DIY stores
  - Powder and ready mixed paints, brushes, palettes or jam tart tins, sprays, pipettes, spoons
  - Felt pens, crayons, pastels
  - Papers of different colours
  - Special papers such as tissues, crêpe, foil
  - Coloured fabrics

- ▷ Magazines and catalogues with coloured pictures
- ▷ Ingredients for dough
- ▷ Food colourings (get big quantities from www.TTS.co.uk)
- ▷ Cellophane or coloured gels
- ▷ Cameras, Dictaphones, video cameras

- ▶ Now experiment with colour mixing, using hands, fingers and sponges or 'dabbers'.
  - ▷ Let the children mix their own paints in old jam tart tins or small palettes, using a variety of brush thicknesses. They may need help to start with, but once they get the hang of it they will be much more confident.
  - ▷ Encourage talk as they work, naming colours, predicting what will happen, and talking about the results.
  - ▷ Try mixing colours by putting a spoonful each of two paints on a table top and letting the children use their hands to mix the colours together.
  - ▷ Make up names for the new colours you make – sandy yellow, grassy green, princess pink, superhero scarlet etc. Look at some shade cards for ideas.
  - ▷ Use the paint you have mixed together to make big patterns and pictures on huge sheets of paper on the floor or on the path or wall outside.
  - ▷ As the children get more confident with mixing their own paint, let them do this for any painting activity, talking about the colours they need before they start.

NB: Some food colourings and paint stain skin and clothing. Make sure children are well protected and warn parents that children's hands may get stained. Moisturising their hands first with a little baby oil or non-perfumed moisturiser will help when removing the colours from skin.

Further questions and provocations

- Discuss with the children how they can make different colours – purple, green, grey, pink. Let them experiment to find out.
- Download some pictures of tropical fish, tropical birds, jewels, leaves and flowers and use these to inspire work with colours.
- Put up some big sheets of paper or a shower curtain outside, and use small sponge rollers and paint to roll paths of different colours all over the paper.
- Experiment with black and white, adding these colours a bit at a time to primary colours (red, blue, yellow) to make darker and darker or paler and paler shades.
- Add food colouring to dough, predicting what the colours will be before you add it.
- Mix paint or food colouring into shaving foam or use finger paints to make prints.

The second exploration:

Go on a shapes and patterns walk

- If you are working with younger children it is wise to keep the two concepts separate so that they work on one at a time.
- Use the resources in your setting to make collections of shapes and patterns.
- Collect baskets of items of unusual shapes as well as the more common ones.
- Get some wrapping paper or wallpaper samples and look at these together, finding patterns and repeats. Then use objects or sponge shapes to make your own versions with colour themes. You could wallpaper the home corner and give it a new colour scheme!
- Make colour, shape and pattern books with your photos. Children will love a Spotty Book, a Stripy Book or a Zigzag Book.

- Look in rummage sales and charity shops for fabrics with unusual colours, patterns and designs – spots, stripes, little pictures, circles, zigzags etc. Look for unusual colours too – lime green, purple, bright yellow, black patent etc. You can use them as role-play clothes, photograph them or cut them up and use the fabric. Keep the interest in colour going as you add shape and pattern.
- Collect cartons and other packaging materials that have interesting shapes. Gift boxes, packaging from snacks, food and drinks will give you lots of ideas. Younger children need to start with simple shapes such as square, circle, rectangle and triangle. Older children will be adding star, oval, sphere, cube etc.
- Explore making all sorts of patterns with paint, felt pen, crayon, with fingers, brushes and other mark makers.
- Use kitchen implements to make patterns on paper or in rolled out dough.
- Get some cookie cutters and use these to cut shapes in dough or clay.

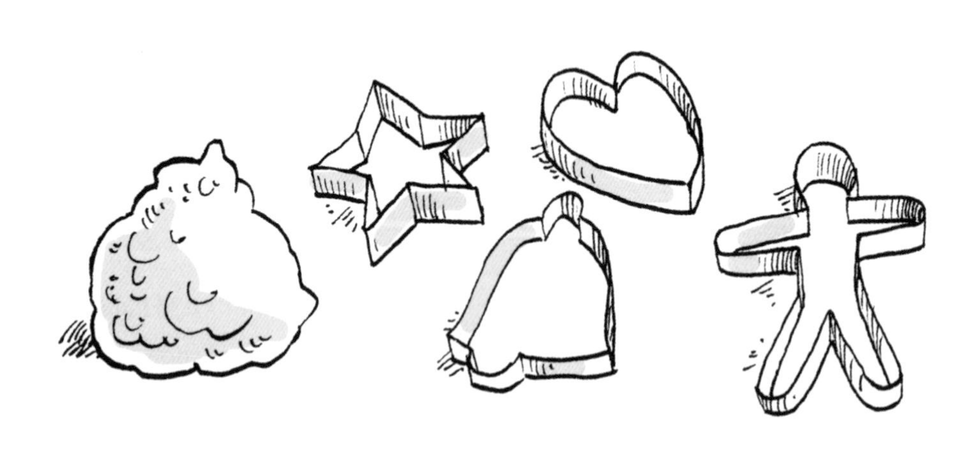

Further questions and provocations

- Can you make a new colour?
- Can you tell me three things that have stripes/dots or spots?
- What is the best colour to wear to a party?
- Why do witches wear black clothes?
- How could you turn a white tee shirt pink?
- Do all trees have green leaves?
- Which animals can change colour?
- What happened when Elmer got wet?
- Can you say a colour pattern like red, blue, red, blue?
- How could we find out everyone's favourite pattern?
- How could you make dotty paper?

Books and stories

- What Colour are your Knickers? Sam Lloyd; Gullane
- Colour; Ella Doran; Tate Publishing
- Shape; Zoe Miller; Tate Publishing
- A is for Artist; Ella Doran; Tate Publishing
- The Little Book of Colour, Shape and Number; Clare Beswick, Featherstone, an imprint of Bloomsbury Publishing Plc
- Mixed-Up Chameleon; Eric Carle; Puffin
- Chameleon's Crazy Colours; Nicola Grant; Little Tigers
- Red Rockets and Rainbow Jelly; Sue Heap; Puffin
- Mr Rabbit and the Lovely Present; Charlotte Zolotow; Red Fox
- All the Colours of the Earth; Sheila Hamanaka; William Morrow
- Brown Bear, Brown Bear What Do You See?; Eric Carle; Puffin
- Elmer; David McKee; Andersen Press
- Two Can Toucan; David McKee; Andersen Press
- Rainbow Fish; Mike Pfister; North South Books

- Pants and More Pants; Nick Sharratt, Picture Corgi
- Aliens Love Underpants; Claire Freedman, Simon and Schuster
- The Shape Game; Anthony Browne; Corgi
- Spotted Yellow Frogs; Matthew van Fleet; Dial Books
- Spots, Stripes or Diamonds; Patricia Stockland; Picture Window

This exploration contributes to the following Goals for the EYFS:

PRIME

Communication and Language ① ③
Physical Development ① ②
PSED ① ② ③

SPECIFIC

Mathematics ① ②
Understanding of the World ① ② ③
Expressive arts and design ① ②

The exploration will also contribute to the Characteristics of Effective Learning:

Playing and exploring

Active learning

Creating and thinking critically

Explore water, rain and ice

Where does water come from, where does it go?
Focus: Weather/community

In this exploration you could look at rain, rivers and the sea, how we get our water and get rid of it, ecological aspects of water preservation and safety. You can also expand into looking at ice, snow and other forms in which water appears.

Talking time

You could wait for a rainy day to start this exploration. Go out in the rain or look out of the window, then talk about what rain is, and how it helps us. What is it made from? What do we need it for?

As you talk, make an ideas map together and note what the children already know and what they want to find out. Here are some starter ideas for your discussion – you will be able to add more.

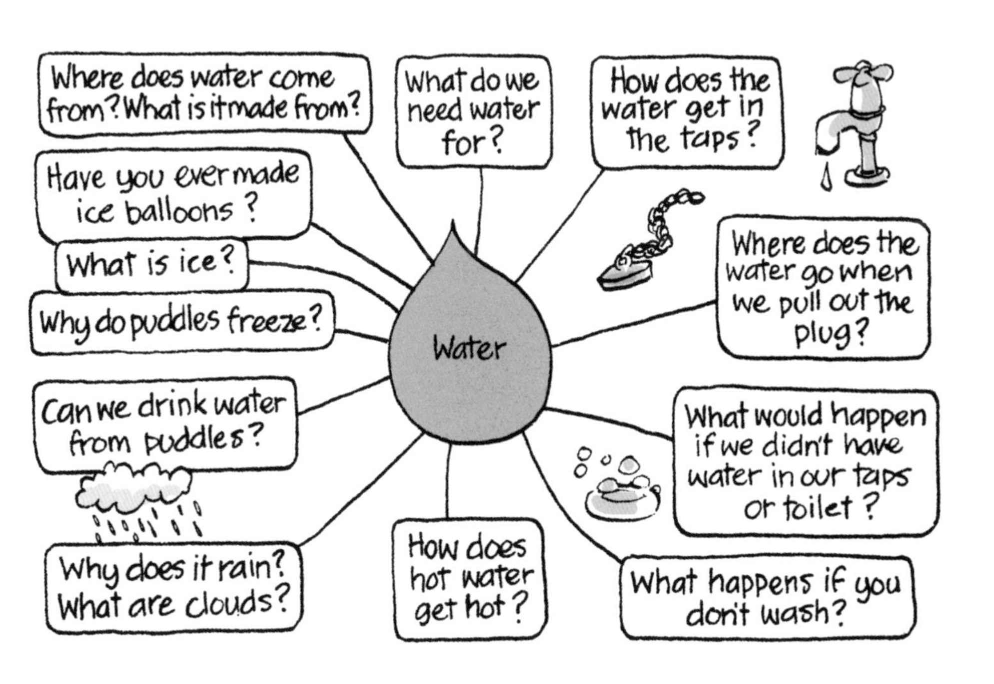

The first exploration:

- **Put some water in your water tray** and look at it together, without any tools or equipment. Find out what it does, how it looks on your hands and fingers, and how it behaves when you scoop it up or drip it from your hands.
- **Now lift your hands out of the water** and watch how the water moves as it falls from your hands, and how your hands get dry, even when you don't use a towel. Talk about what 'waterproof' means.
- **Now talk about what you will need to explore water and rain**, and what you want to find out. Make a 'getting ready' list. Here are some things the children might suggest, or you might consider collecting:
  - Boots and waterproof clothing
  - Umbrellas
  - Buckets and other containers
  - Guttering and drainpipes (try to get some foam lagging or protection for pipes from a builder's merchant)
  - Jars, plastic bottles, other containers
  - Plastic funnels, sprays, plastic tubing, pipettes and syringes
  - Sponges, paintbrushes, sponge rollers
  - Food colouring and paints
  - Cameras – take photos of all your water explorations and get the children to do so too

After your first exploration:

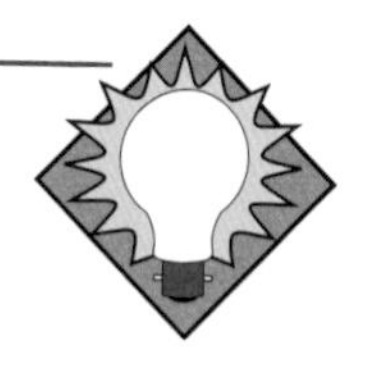

- Use a story about water or rain to continue the interest – Mrs Wishy Washy or Mr Gumpy's Outing would be good ones to start with. Or look at a non-fiction book about water such as Drips and Drops.
- Sort your equipment into baskets or trays, so the children can find the things they need and still keep the water tray uncluttered.
- Offer all sorts of equipment for exploring water in bowls and water trays. This is a good outdoor activity, as you don't need to worry about spills.
- When it rains, go out together in small groups and explore puddles. Drop things in the water, float leaves and sticks, and watch ripples. You could add things to puddles – colouring, mud, gravel or even float a bit of cooking oil on the surface and watch the colours as the oil expands.
- Watch drips and drops as they run down windows and doors, guessing which drop will win the race.
- Watch the rainwater running down drainpipes and into drains. Float small objects such as twigs on the rainwater in gutters and watch them disappear down gratings and drain covers.

On rainy days:

- Leave buckets and bowls to catch the rain. Use the rain to wash wheeled toys or water the plants.
- Make little boats from junk and recycled materials such as corks and bits of balsa wood. Float these in puddles and pools or gutters.
- Look at waterproofing, shelters and keeping dry.

On other outdoor days:

- Fix some guttering to a fence, add a funnel at the top, and pour water into the funnel.
- Paint with water or liquid mud, using brushes of all sizes and sponges, scrapers and rollers to cover the walls, floors and fences of your setting.
- Provide water in a big camping container with a tap. Fit it with a hose and let children help themselves to use as petrol for wheeled vehicles or car washes, for making tea (not for drinking), for filling waterways or adding to sand and dough mixtures.

- Help the children to make a waterway in your outdoor area, using plastic and foam guttering, drainpipes and other found materials. Prop the waterway on big bricks or crates so the water flows. Float little plastic or wooden boats down the waterway and watch to see how they go.
- Provide a whole range of natural and manufactured objects for floating and sinking experiments, in independent play or for adult-led 'playful science' as you ask open questions and think along with them.
- Add water to extend your usual range of malleable and tactile materials, such as sand, cornflour, clay, sawdust and compost into new experiences.
- Offer an outdoor role-play experience that uses water – fire-fighters, a car wash, a petrol station, all with real water.
- Make water music on metal surfaces and with instruments such as triangles and bells. Add some drums, buckets or plastic bowls for a musical thunderstorm!
- Help the children to make a pond in a half-barrel or a plastic water tank. Remember to put netting over the top if you are working with very young children. Watch to see if any birds, insects or animals come to your pond.

Some adult-initiated activities:

- Use water in food preparation and simple cooking:
  - Food that doesn't need cooking, just water – such as ice lollies, instant noodles, jelly, couscous or Bulgar wheat;
  - Easy cook foods that only need a microwave – such as custard made from dried milk powder, or easy cake mixes for the microwave. You can now get pancake mixture in a bottle that only needs milk (make this from milk and water).
- Go for a 'water walk' round your setting and garden and take photos of everywhere you find water – the toilets, the kitchen, the shower, the staffroom, the radiators, outside taps, drains and water pipes, and all the machines that use water – the dishwasher, washing machine, kettle, water heater, water fountain or water machine. Use these as talking points about where water comes from, where it goes and why it is so important to people, animals and plants.

- Look at all the photos you have taken of water explorations, and use these to make a display, a book or a PowerPoint presentation, asking the children what they want to say about each photo.
- Explore the weather:
  - Make weather charts. Download some weather symbols from the Internet, laminate these and stick them on the chart.
  - Look up 'rain gauge' on the Internet to find out how to make a simple rain gauge with the children
  - Make a role-play TV by cutting a screen in the front of a cardboard box, and 'broadcast' the weather forecast. Some children may need you to model this!
- Explore ice:
  - Make big blocks of ice in plastic containers, and tip these into the water tray for children to explore.
  - Make ice balloons by freezing balloons filled with water (adding colouring and putting small objects such as beads, sequins, tinsel or tiny toys inside if you wish). When the balloons are frozen, let the children break the balloons to reveal the ice balls inside and watch them melt, releasing their treasure. They will melt more quickly if you float them in water, or put them in the sun.

Extensions into child-initiated learning (stimuli for children who are interested in replaying the experience):

- Make a seaside, either a real one for barefoot play, or a small world one in the water tray with Play people and seaside props such as cocktail umbrellas.
- Let children experiment with mixing water and other safe substances such as paste powder, flour, cornflour, tea bags, food colouring, clay or sand. Stay with them and talk about what is happening and whether they can get the water out again.
- Provide the equipment and resources to mix their own paint and make their own simple dough recipes.
- Help them to squeeze fruit to make fruit juices and fruit ice-lollies.
- Buy a waterway kit for experiments – from Asco, Brio or TTS.

And together you could find out about water, rain and ice by looking at or downloading some images from Google, or visiting some websites.

Google searches – water, house plan, water system, plumbing, toilet, WC, clean water, reservoir, rain, river, water wheel – ice, ice cave, ice carving, ice sculpture, Ice hotel, ice skating, frozen waterfall, frozen in ice, ice shapes, ice balloons – rain, raindrop, puddle, stream, drain, flood, pond, desert

Websites – www.ltscotland.org.uk/earlyyears/.../raingauge make a simple rain gauge

http://home.howstuffworks.com/toilet1.htm has a working toilet model!

http://www.exploratorium.edu for a DVD of making ice balloons

http://www.pbase.com/es839145/ice for photos of ice shapes

http://www.videojug.com/film/how-to-make-orange-ice-lollies an amusing little film for children on making their own ice lollies with fresh orange juice

http://www.guardian.co.uk/lifeandstyle/2007/jun/24/foodanddrink.features6 has more ice lolly recipes

http://www.weatherwizkids.com for weather games and experiments

http://www.metoffice.gov.uk/education/kids/weather_station_rain_gauge.html make your own weather station, games and printable sheets

http://www.stickersandcharts.com/weather.php for free printable weather chart stickers

http://www.bbc.co.uk/cbeebies/balamory/makes/weatherchart/ make a simple spinner weather chart

Further experiences and visits to keep the interest alive:

- Keep your weather chart going and log all the rainy days.
- Do some experiments with plants and see what happens if you don't give them any water.
- Get some big plastic lids or shallow containers and make patterns of natural objects (leaves, petals, little stones, seeds etc.) in the bottom of these. Gently pour a shallow layer of water over the pattern, freeze it in your freezer (or outside on a very cold night) and then lift your ice patterns carefully out of the moulds and look at them against a light.
- Freeze bird food in containers of water and hang these up to melt for the birds in winter.
- Take small paintbrushes out on a frosty morning to write and make patterns in frosty surfaces on fences and the ground.
- Freeze water in unusual containers – rubber gloves, Wellington boots, plastic zip-lock bags, jelly moulds etc. Be imaginative – anything you can fill with water and fit in the freezer will make fascinating shapes. Add some small items to the water if you wish, and when they have frozen, tip or shake them out in a water tray with or without water in it.
- Make up a dance about water and weather, with water music from suitable instruments including shakers, rain sticks and bells. Some children could make the music while others dance.
- Use a paddling pool for paddling or for water play such as fishing games, catching numbers words, shapes or just fish in little nets. Older children could score their games on a white board.
- Go out for a walk on a rainy day. Play 'Pooh sticks' under a bridge or down a gutter. Splash in puddles and enjoy getting wet. Then come back, dry off and snuggle under a soft blanket for a story about the rain.

Further questions and provocations

- What would happen if it never rained again?
- How could we make a place to play outside on rainy days?
- Where does the rainwater go after it goes down the drain?
- When puddles dry up, where does the rain go?
- What is a water wheel? Could you make one?
- How could you make bath water clean again?
- What happens if you don't wash?
- Do animals and birds have baths?
- Can you think of a way to make water go uphill?
- What is dew?
- What are clouds made of? What is above the clouds?
- How could you stop a flood?

Books and stories

- Clean and Healthy; Angela Royston, Heinemann
- Making Water Clean; Rebecca Olien; First Facts
- The Drop Goes Plop; Sam Goodwin; Wayland
- Science with Water; Helen Edom; Usborne
- The Drop in my Drink; Meredith Hooper; Frances Lincoln
- Whatever the Weather; Karen Wallace; Dorling Kindersley
- The Little Book of Sand and Water; Sally Featherstone; Featherstone, an imprint of Bloomsbury Publishing Plc
- The Little Book of Outside in all Weathers; Sally Featherstone; Featherstone, an imprint of Bloomsbury Publishing Plc
- Hidden Under the Ground: The World Beneath Your Feet by Peter Kent; Dutton
- Doing the Washing; Sarah Garland; Frances Lincoln
- Washing; Gwenyth Swain; Zero to Ten
- Living in the Arctic; Allan Fowler; Children's Press
- Matsumara's Ice Sculptures; Anna Prokos; Longman
- Winter; Monica Hughes; Raintree
- Nature's Playground; Fiona Danks; Francis Lincoln

- Where Do They Go When it Rains?; Gerda Muller; Floris
- Rain; Jessica Manya Stojic; Dragonfly

- Weatherwatch - Rain; Honor Head; QED
- Weather; Catriona Clarke; Usborne Beginners
- Water and the Weather; Rebecca Ollen; First Facts
- I Like Ice Cream; Robin Pickering; Children's Press
- Freezing and Melting; Robin Nelson; Lerner
- Ice Bear; Nicola Davies; Walker Books

- The Emperor's Egg; Martin Jenkins; Walker Books
- Penguin Small; Mick Inkpen; Hodder
- Tiger in the Snow; Nick Butterworth; HarperCollins
- The Snowman; Raymond Briggs; Puffin
- Winnie in Winter; Valerie Thomas; OUP
- Alfie's Weather; Shirley Hughes; Red Fox
- Topsy and Tim, Red Boots, Yellow Boots; Gareth Adamson; Ladybird
- Raindrop Plop; Wendy Lewison; Viking
- Rabbits and Raindrops; Jim Arnosky; Puffin
- Noah's Ark; Lucy Cousins; Walker

This exploration contributes to the following Goals for the EYFS:

PRIME

Communication and Language ① ③
Physical Development ① ②
PSED ① ② ③

SPECIFIC

Mathematics ① ②
Understanding of the World ① ② ③
Expressive arts and design ① ②

The exploration will also contribute to the Characteristics of Effective Learning:

Playing and exploring

Active learning

Creating and thinking critically

Explore food and growing things

Where do potatoes come from? Focus: Food plants

This investigation is about food and where it comes from. Growing potatoes is a simple way to keep interest over a period, and you can introduce it simply by bringing a bag of potatoes to your setting.

Talking time

Talk about the potatoes you have brought, handle them, smell them and cut some open to look inside. Ask some simple questions: Where do potatoes grow? Do they grow on trees or on a plant? Do they have leaves? How do we like to eat them?

As you talk, make an ideas map together and note what the children already know and what they want to find out. Here are some starter ideas for discussion – you will be able to think of more.

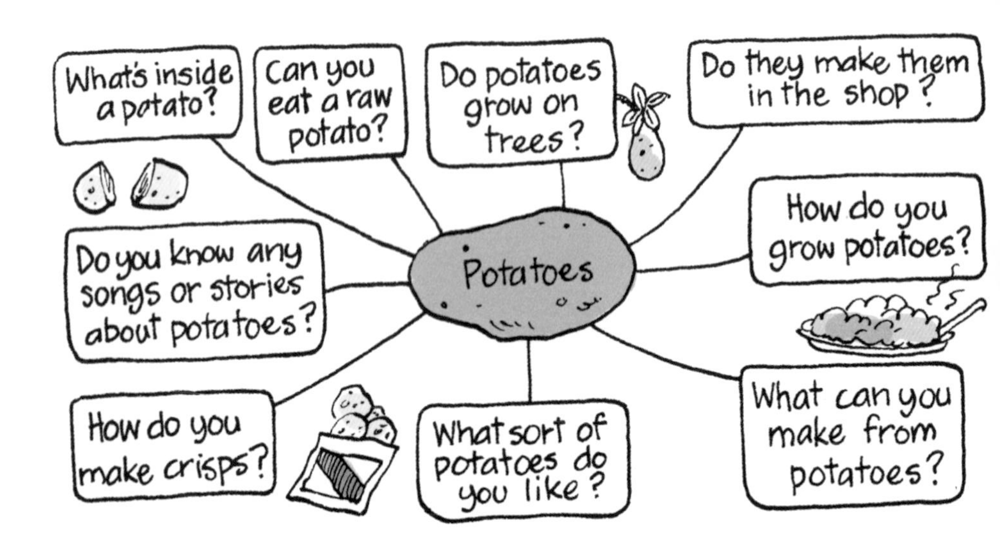

The first exploration:

I will need

You may want to time this exploration so you can use the resources and other links on http://www.potatoesforschools.org.uk/ which is a great site for schools. If you do, they recommend that you buy seed potatoes from a garden centre and start at a particular time of year.

- **Look carefully at your potatoes**. You could give each child a potato to look at and talk about. Look at the details of the skin and the little 'eyes' where the shoots grow.
- **Download some photos** of potatoes growing and look at these with the children, enter 'potatoes growing photos' in Google and download or print some of plants and growing shoots as well as harvested potatoes.
- **Cut some of the remaining potatoes** in half and look inside.
- **Now ask the children** if they would like to grow their potato into a new potato plant. What do the children think you need? They may suggest some of these:
  - Soil or earth
  - Water
  - Pots or other containers
  - Trowels or spades
- **You will also need:**
  - Empty egg boxes to put the potatoes in to start them off. This is called 'chitting'.
  - A grow bag or some cheap buckets, big plastic plant pots or plastic boxes. Our method uses buckets; but a grow bag is fine; a cheap, clean way of managing compost which has room for plenty of potatoes.
  - You will also need some more compost to cover the shoots as they grow. This is called 'earthing up'.
  - A camera.
- **Before you start to grow your potatoes**, take some photos and let the children draw or paint pictures of their own potato, so they can record the growth.

Stage 1 – Chitting the potatoes

- When the children have looked at and recorded their first look at potatoes, talk about what you need to do to start the potatoes growing. Help them to put each potato in a space in an egg box. If they want to name their own potato, ask them for ideas of how they could do this.
- Leave the potatoes somewhere light and warm for about ten days, checking them every day. They will soon start to grow shoots from the 'eyes' in their skins.

While you wait:

- Take time every day to watch what is happening to the potatoes.
- You can handle the potatoes gently but make sure the children know that they are growing, and the shoots will break very easily.
- Talk about the shoots and how they are growing up towards the light.

More about potatoes and simple cooking:

- While the potatoes are growing their shoots, you can start to find out more about potatoes. You could:
  - Read some stories about potatoes.
  - Use some real potatoes to play and sing 'One Potato, Two Potato'.
  - Use potatoes to make potato soup, mashed potatoes or simple oven potato crisps.
  - Make some jacket potatoes or oven chips for snack time.
  - Make this edible potato play dough, which is easy enough for children to help with. To make enough dough for a group, you need:

    20 large potatoes

    6 medium eggs

    6 cups of self raising flour.

    Wash, peel, and grate the RAW potatoes and put in a bowl. Add the other ingredients and mix well to make a firm dough. Pat or roll with clean hands and make into shapes or patties. Put on a greased baking sheet and cook in a hot oven for 30-45 minutes until golden brown.

Stage 2 – Planting the potatoes

- In about ten to fourteen days the potatoes should have grown strong, firm shoots and will be ready for planting.
- You need some cheap buckets and something sharp to make holes in the bottom of each one for drainage.
- The potatoes need to finish growing in a bright place outside, but you will need to bring them in if there is a frost or to protect them from other damage.
- Fill the buckets two-thirds full with compost (or the contents of a grow bag) and let each child plant their own potato by pressing it gently into the soil with the shoots pointing up. You should be able to get between three and five potatoes in each bucket, so make sure you buy enough buckets!
- Cover the potatoes, filling the bucket nearly to the top with compost.
- It's a good idea to plant an extra bucket so you can dig some up to look at as they grow.
- Keep the buckets damp, water them if it doesn't rain, but don't water too much or the potatoes will rot.
- Take photos of each stage of this planting activity.

Stage 3 – Watching the potatoes

- Watch your potatoes as they grow, taking photos, drawing pictures, and talking about them as they grow stems, leaves and flowers. If you gently dig up a potato plant you will see the roots, and eventually you will see tiny tubers growing among the roots.
- Once the potatoes have flowered, the leaves will begin to shrivel and go brown. STOP watering now, and wait two weeks for the potatoes to finish growing.

Stage 4 – Harvesting the potatoes

- Your potatoes should now be ready to harvest. Let the children dig up their own potatoes and look at what they have grown!

Some adult-initiated activities:

- Help the children to weigh the potatoes.
- Invent a dance based on the idea of a growing potato plant.
- Talk about how you could cook the potatoes and eat them. The potatoes will taste wonderful if you just wash them and boil them, but you could make potato cakes or oven chips.
- Make some of your photos into displays, books or PowerPoint presentations so children can sequence and recall the experience.
- Get parents involved in planting bulbs and seeds for next year.
- Try 'The Little Book of Growing Things' (Featherstone, an imprint of Bloomsbury Publishing Plc).

Extensions into child-initiated learning (stimuli for children who are interested in replaying the experience):

- Provide the equipment for role-play cooking or shopping with potatoes (your own or a new bag from the shop).
- Provide child size (but real) garden tools, a place to dig and some seeds to plant.
- Offer some potatoes and objects to press in to make a Mr or Mrs Potato Head.
- Offer books and songs about growing things, gardens and food to catch children's interests.
- Add some plant, seed and bulb catalogues to your print resources. Let the children choose some bulbs or seeds to order, or just cut out the pictures for home made books and collages.

Further experiences and visits to keep the interest alive:

- Provide pots, compost and some different seeds for planting in containers or in your garden. Lettuce, carrots, radishes all grow quickly and are fairly reliable. If you haven't got a garden, grow cress in containers or beans in jars.
- Visit a garden centre and look at food plants such as fruit trees, strawberry plants, or beans and peas.
- Make a garden centre role-play area in your setting with real or pretend flowers and plants.
- Plant containers and hanging baskets with vegetables or colourful annual plants to brighten up your setting and maintain the children's interest in gardening.
- Make gardening part of your planning every month and every year.

And together you could find out about potatoes by looking at or downloading some images from Google, or visiting some websites.

Google searches – potatoes, potatoes growing, potatoes underground, potato field, potato picking, potato picking machine, planting potatoes, making chips, making crisps, fish and chips, mashed potato

Websites – http://www.potatoesforschools.org.uk/ is a brilliant site where you can find out how to grow your own potatoes in a school or setting. It has everything you need, including instructions, PowerPoint presentations, DVD, information and even a potato webcam!

http://www.burtschips.com - a cartoon model of a chip-making machine

http://www.teachers.tv/videos/crisps - a good DVD of the process of making chips from field to bag

http://simplyrecipes.com/recipes/oven-fried_potato_chips has a simple recipe for oven baked potato chips.

Books and stories

- Oliver's Vegetables; Vivian French; Hodder
- Eddie's Garden; Sarah Garland; Frances Lincoln
- Jim and the Beanstalk; Puffin; Raymond Briggs
- The Little Book of Growing Things; Sally Featherstone; Featherstone, an imprint of Bloomsbury Publishing Plc
- How a Seed Grows; Helene Jordan; Collins
- Potatoes; Joyce Bentley; Chrysalis
- Potatoes (Grow Your Own); Helen Lanz; Franklin Watts
- Eating Fruit and Vegetables; Claire Llewellyn; Collins
- What If We Grew Our Own Food? (CD and photo Pack); Featherstone/A C Black
- Grow it, Eat it; Dorling Kindersley
- Grow it, Cook it with Kids; Amanda Grant; Ryland, Peters and Small
- The Enormous Potato; Aubrey Davis; Kids Can Press

This exploration contributes to the following Goals for the EYFS:

PRIME

Communication and Language ① ③
Physical Development ① ②
PSED ① ② ③

SPECIFIC

Mathematics ① ②
Understanding of the World ① ② ③
Expressive arts and design ① ②

The exploration will also contribute to the Characteristics of Effective Learning:

Playing and exploring

Active learning

Creating and thinking critically

Explore minibeasts

What are minibeasts? Focus: Animal life

This exploration is a good one to start in the summer or autumn, when insects and other minibeasts are plentiful. If you continue your explorations throughout the year, you can track changes, look at habitats and explore life cycles throughout the year, revisiting the places where your local minibeasts live.

Talking time

Talk about minibeasts, maybe starting with a story such as the Very Hungry Caterpillar or The Snail and the Whale. Talk with the children about the very small creatures that live near us, even though we don't always see them. Ask some questions such as: What is a minibeast? Where could we find some? What do they eat?

As you talk, make an ideas map together and note what the children already know and what they want to find out. Here are some starter ideas for discussion – you will be able to think of more!

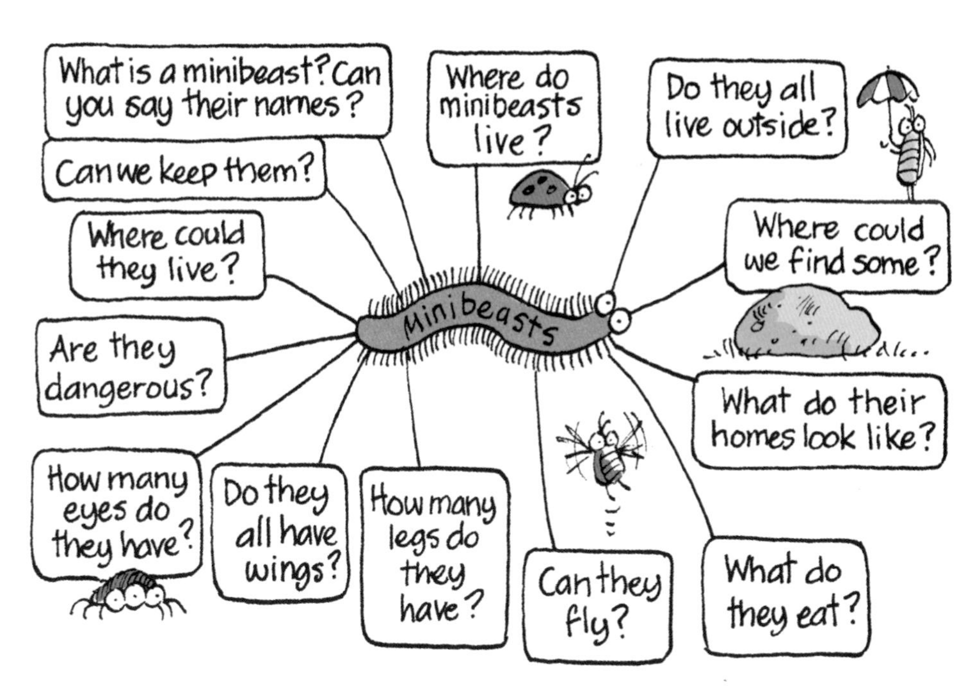

Preparing for your exploration:

- You could start this exploration by making up and singing a new version of an old rhyme – 'The Bear Hunt'. This can become the 'Bug Hunt' by substituting a few words and new places:

  We're going on a bug hunt,
  We're going to catch some small ones,
  What a beautiful day, we're not scared!

- Talk about what you need to take, and what you want to find out. Make a 'getting ready' list. Here are some things the children might suggest, or you might consider taking:
  - Bug hunters or 'pooters'
  - Magnifying glasses
  - Small plastic bottles or jars with tops
  - A plastic box for bigger finds
  - Cameras
  - Scissors to snip some leaves for minibeast food
  - A trowel to dig up some soil or turf
  - Antiseptic spray or hand wipes
  - Sting relief for nettle stings
  - A book about bugs

- Some children may be anxious or even frightened of insects, others may want to squash or stamp on them. Take time to talk about this and acknowledge fears but tell children that cruelty, even to small creatures, is unacceptable.

- Make sure right from the start that the children understand about exploring living things. Explain that they must treat them with care and respect, returning minibeasts to the place they were found when the children have finished looking at them.

The first exploration:

- **Take a walk in your outdoor area**, asking the children where they think you should look for minibeasts – under leaves and logs, behind sheds, under stones or rocks, on leaves and flowers, on the bark of trees, or the back of leaves.
- **Look carefully at the minibeasts** you find, carefully picking them up or scooping them into bug boxes, where the children can look at them closely. If you find an insect or other bug that you don't recognise, make sure you look it up before capturing or handling it.
- **Some minibeasts** such as woodlice, worms, caterpillars, slugs and snails move very slowly and are ideal for a first exploration. Start with these and let children get used to looking at them, before handling them.
- **Ladybirds and other small beetles** are plentiful and children love watching them. Spiders of all sizes will delight children as they watch them safely enclosed in a bug box.
- **Flying creatures** such as flies, mosquitoes, butterflies and moths are very fragile, so it is best to just photograph these when you see them on your walk.

When you get back you could:

- Carefully put your bugs and minibeasts in a plastic aquarium with plenty of the wood, leaves and soil you found near them. Cover the aquarium to stop them escaping – even slow moving creatures such as slugs can do a lot of damage to your displays and resources, rasping their way across paper and books! Children can watch the minibeasts as they move about in their habitat.

- Find a piece of Perspex or thick plastic from a picture frame, and put some slugs or snails on the surface. Carefully lift the Perspex and you will be able to see how the slugs and snails move across it. If you put leaves or lettuce near them, you can also see their mouths as they eat.
- Look at books and tell stories about minibeasts (see Books and stories section).
- Have a snail race on a smooth surface or some black paper (which will let you see the silver trails they make).
- Look at your photos and make them into a book or PowerPoint presentation to show parents, or to look at in your setting.
- Make a minibeast-themed role-play area:
  - Set up a tent and collect binoculars, backpacks and hats for an 'Explorers' Camp'.
  - Use small world minibeasts, branches and leaves to make a small world habitat.
  - If you have a computer compatible microscope, set up a science lab with white coats, where children can watch (but not experiment on) the minibeasts you have found.

Some adult-initiated activities:

- Provide plenty of pictures and books for children to make their own drawings and paintings of minibeasts.
- Use minibeast finger puppets to tell stories and sing songs.
- Make books of photos or drawings of the minibeasts you have found.
- Go on further minibeast hunts at different times of day, in different weathers and in different seasons.
- Make minibeast mini-books with just a few pages where children can record the minibeasts they find.

Extensions into child-initiated learning (stimuli for children who are interested in replaying the experience):

- Provide plenty of equipment for more bug-hunting as part of free choice play.
- Get some carpet squares and let the children sit or lie on these to watch ants and other minibeasts in the garden.
- Offer magnifying glasses and hand-held microscopes for free observation.
- Provide some clear containers with lids so children can watch the minibeasts they find without harming them.

And together you could find out about minibeasts by looking at or downloading some images from Google, or visiting some websites.

Google searches – 'minibeasts Foundation Stage' for lots of websites and ideas;

Google images – minibeasts, snails, slugs, butterfly, moth, caterpillar, fly, ladybird, wormery, ant farm, ant hill, beetle

Websites – http://animals.pppst.com/minibeasts.html for ideas, games and PowerPoint presentations

www.teachers.ash.org.au/.../minibeasts/minibeasts.htm has links to lots of information

www.galaxy.bedfordshire.gov.uk/.../animals_minibeasts.htm library site with lots of useful links

http://www.british-trees.com – the Woodland Trust – tree pictures, free charts & ideas for activities for children in the Nature Detectives section

http://www.insectlore-europe.com/butterflies.html has live butterfly eggs to hatch in your school or setting

http://www.thekidsgarden.co.uk/MakingAWormery.html for simple instructions on making a wormery

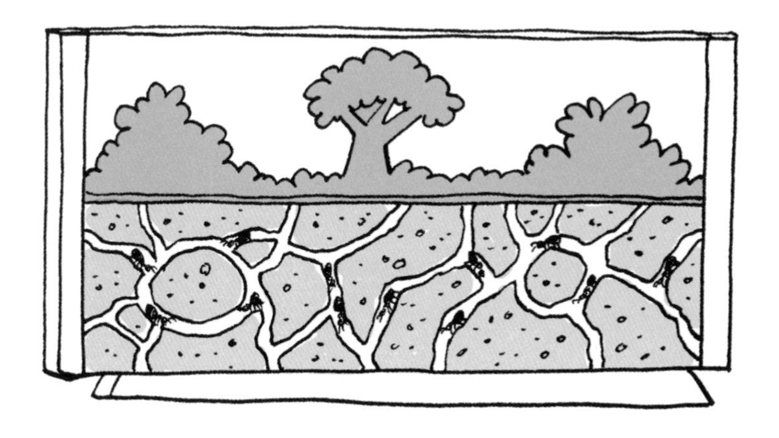

Further experiences to keep the interest alive:

- Make a wormery.
  - You need a deep transparent container such as a pasta or sweet jar. You also need some soil, sand, newspaper and some worms.
  - Cover the outside of the jar with black paper so the worms think they are still underground.
  - Now dig up some soil and some worms. Put the worms carefully in a bucket or bowl while you fill the wormery.
  - Put a layer of damp sand in the bottom of the jar, then a layer of shredded newspaper, then a layer of soil. Repeat the layers.
  - Add the worms and put some vegetable waste (lettuce leaves, potato peelings) on the surface and put the covered container somewhere warm for a few days before looking under the covering to see what the worms have done.
  - Don't keep the wormery for more than a couple of weeks before returning the worms to the wild.
- Contact a butterfly supplier such as Insect Lore and obtain some butterflies to hatch and release in your garden. This is a really wonderful way to experience wildlife in close up, and children will be delighted to watch the caterpillars and then release their own butterflies.
- Make an ant farm.
  - You need a transparent glass or plastic bowl (a plastic aquarium is ideal). You also need another container that will fit inside the aquarium. This is to encourage the ants to make their tunnels where the children can see them.
  - You also need some soil, and some ants. Look for an ants' nest and collect ants, a queen (they have wings) and some of the little white eggs if you can find them. The children can collect black ants, but remember, red ants STING!
  - Dig up some soil and pour it between the two layers of the ant farm. Now add the ants and cover the top securely so the ants can't escape.
  - Cover the whole container with black paper to let the ants start to build their tunnels.

- ▷ Leave the ant farm for several days before uncovering it to see what has happened. The ants should have made tunnels and burrows where you can see them.

- If you have younger children, they may be happy just to have a little transparent box with a few leaves and one or two ants to watch immediately and closely, letting them go again after a few minutes.
- Plant some flowers and bushes that attract butterflies – Buddleia is a very good choice of a shrub that grows quickly and is guaranteed to attract insects.
- Go pond dipping in a supervised area to look for minibeasts that live in water.
- Find out about bees and how they make honey. Have a Teddy Bears' Picnic with honey sandwiches or honey cakes.
- Explore habitats, homes and holes where insects live. Make an insect home by filling a food can with short lengths of bamboo, straws or hollow twigs. Hang it up in your garden and bugs will come to shelter in it during the winter.

Further questions and provocations

- How could we get more butterflies to come to our garden?
- Where do worms sleep?
- Do all caterpillars turn into butterflies?
- Do beetles, slugs and snails all lay eggs?
- Could we make a place for spiders to live in our garden?
- Which minibeasts live indoors?
- Do spiders really hurt you?
- Which minibeasts sting? Which ones bite?
- How many legs do minibeasts have? Do they all have the same number of legs?
- Which insects come out at night?
- Where do insects go in winter?
- What sort of insects would live in a tree? How many different sorts would be there?

Books and stories

- The Very Hungry Caterpillar, The Bad Tempered Ladybird, and The Very Busy Spider; all by Eric Carle; Puffin
- The Little Book of Minibeast Hotels; Ann Roberts; Featherstone, an imprint of Bloomsbury Publishing Plc
- Minibeasts (I wonder why); Karen Wallace; Kingfisher
- AARRGGH, Spider; Lydia Monks; Egmont
- Minibeasts (Hot topics); Gerald Legg; Belitha Press
- Minibeasts; Nancy Dickman; Collins Big Cats
- From Caterpillar to Butterfly; Deborah Heiligman; HarperCollins
- Wiggling Worms at Work; Wendy Pfeffer; Harper Trophy
- Yucky Worms; Vivian French; Walker
- Slugs and Snails; Sally Morgan; Belitha PressMinibeasts,
- Going on a Bug Hunt; Stewart Ross; Franklin Watts
- What's Under the Log?; Anne Hunter; Houghton Mifflin
- The Where to Find Minibeasts series (new in 2010); Sarah Ridley; Franklin Watts:
  - Minibeasts under a Stone
  - Minibeasts on a Plant
  - Minibeasts in the Home
  - Minibeasts in the Soil
  - Minibeasts in a Pond
  - Minibeasts in the Compost Heap

This exploration contributes to the following Goals for the EYFS:

PRIME

Communication and Language ① ③
Physical Development ① ②
PSED ① ② ③

SPECIFIC

Mathematics ① ②
Understanding of the World ① ② ③
Expressive arts and design ① ②

The exploration will also contribute to the Characteristics of Effective Learning:

Playing and exploring

Active learning

Creating and thinking critically

The **Little Books** series consists of:

- All Through the Year
- Bags, Boxes & Trays
- Bricks and Boxes
- Celebrations
- Christmas
- Circle Time
- Clay and Malleable Materials
- Clothes and Fabrics
- Colour, Shape and Number
- Cooking from Stories
- Cooking Together
- Counting
- Dance
- Dance, with music CD
- Discovery Bottles
- Dough
- Fine Motor Skills
- Fun on a Shoestring
- Games with Sounds
- Growing Things
- ICT
- Investigations
- Junk Music
- Language Fun
- Light and Shadow
- Listening
- Living Things
- Look and Listen
- Making Books and Cards
- Making Poetry
- Mark Making
- Maths Activities
- Maths from Stories
- Maths Songs and Games
- Messy Play
- Music
- Nursery Rhymes
- Outdoor Play
- Outside in All Weathers
- Parachute Play
- Persona Dolls
- Phonics
- Playground Games
- Prop Boxes for Role Play
- Props for Writing
- Puppet Making
- Puppets in Stories
- Resistant Materials
- Role Play
- Sand and Water
- Science through Art
- Scissor Skills
- Sewing and Weaving
- Small World Play
- Sound Ideas
- Storyboards
- Storytelling
- Seasons
- Time and Money
- Time and Place
- Treasure Baskets
- Treasureboxes
- Tuff Spot Activities
- Washing Lines
- Writing

All available from

www.bloomsbury.com/featherstone